Massachusetts Free-soil party.

Reunion of the Free Soilers of 1848

At Downer Landing, Hingham, Mass., August 9, 1877 ..

Massachusetts Free-soil party.

Reunion of the Free Soilers of 1848
At Downer Landing, Hingham, Mass., August 9, 1877 ..

ISBN/EAN: 9783744786249

Printed in Europe, USA, Canada, Australia, Japan

Cover: Foto ©ninafisch / pixelio.de

More available books at **www.hansebooks.com**

REUNION

OF THE

FREE-SOILERS OF 1848,

AT

DOWNER LANDING, HINGHAM, MASS.,

AUGUST 9, 1877.

"BEHOLD, THERE ARISETH A LITTLE CLOUD, LIKE A MAN'S HAND."

BOSTON:
ALBERT J. WRIGHT, PRINTER,
79 MILK STREET (CORNER OF FEDERAL).
1877.

REUNION OF THE FREE-SOILERS OF 1848.

The Free-Soil party, organized in 1848, which marked a new era in politics, and prepared the way for the Republican party, which finally triumphed in the Presidential election of 1860, had such an influence upon the history of this country, that the events which led to its formation must ever be of interest, not only to those engaged in the movement, but to the student of politics; and therefore it is deemed important to preserve a record of the proceedings which took place at a reunion of the men who took an active part in the organization and support of that party, which was held at Melville Garden, Hingham, Mass., on the 9th of August, 1877. Hence these pages.

The idea of such a gathering had been in the minds of several gentlemen for some years; but certain circumstances seemed to render it expedient to postpone the meeting for a time, until, finally, Mr. SAMUEL DOWNER took the matter resolutely in hand, and it is mainly to his exertions and liberality that the signal success of the gathering is due. The purpose of the meeting is sufficiently set forth in the opening address of Mr. Downer, and nothing need be said here in that regard.

The following invitation was prepared, and sent to two hundred and twenty gentlemen, who were either active in the campaign of 1848, or whose subsequent connection with the party, or relation to the leaders of that day, gave them a title to be remembered on such an occasion.

"For Auld Lang Syne."

BOSTON, July 19, 1877.

DEAR SIR:—I respectfully invite you to attend a reunion of the Free-Soilers of 1848, at Melville Garden, on Thursday, the ninth day of August.

The boat will leave Rowe's Wharf at 10.30 and 12.15; return at 4, 5.20, and 6.45. Clam-bake at 1.30.

Please inform me whether we may expect the pleasure of your company. I have the honor to be,

Faithfully yours,

SAM'L DOWNER.

The following is a list of the gentlemen invited:—

HON. CHAS. FRANCIS ADAMS,	Quincy.
HON. JOHN B. ALLEY,	Lynn.
WM. ASHBY,	Newburyport.
REV. GEORGE ALLEN,	Worcester.
M. ANAGNOS,	Boston.
FORESTER ANDREW,	Boston.
ALBERT G. BROWNE,	Salem.
JOHN N. BARBOUR,	Boston.
WM. L. BURT,	Boston.
PETER C. BACON,	Worcester.
HON. JOHN D. BALDWIN,	Worcester.
HON. JOHN I. BAKER,	Beverly.
HON. F. W. BIRD,	East Walpole.
THOS. T. BOUVÉ,	Hingham.
HON. JOHN A. BOLLES,	Washington, D. C.
S. H. BENSON,	Streator, Ill.
GEO. WM. BOND,	Boston.
WM. I. BOWDITCH,	Boston.
JONATHAN BATTLES,	Dorchester.
CYRUS BREWER,	Boston.
J. N. BUFFUM,	Lynn.
WINSLOW BATTLES,	Boston.
EBEN BIRD,	Dorchester.
STEPHEN BAKER,	Dorchester.
HON. JAS. A. BRIGGS,	New York City.
MATTHEW BOLLES,	Boston.
ALBERT G. BROWNE, JR.,	New York.
JOHN BOTUME, JR.,	Boston.

CHAS. C. BARRY,	Boston.
EDWARD S. BUFFUM,	Chelsea.
WM. WELLS BROWN,	Boston.
GEO. BRADBURN,	Boston.
JOHN R. BREWER,	Hingham.
CHAS. B. BARNES,	Boston.
H. O. BRIGGS,	Boston.
H. W. BLANCHARD,	Neponset.
SETH L. BURR,	Hingham Centre.
NATHAN BURR,	Hingham Centre.
Dr. HENRY I. BOWDITCH,	Boston.
ALVAH A. BURRAGE,	Boston.
ASAPH CHURCHILL,	Boston.
Hon. HENRY CHAPIN,	Worcester.
THEOPHILUS CHANDLER,	Brookline.
Hon. WM. CLAFLIN,	Boston.
Hon. J. M. CHURCHILL,	Boston.
CHAS. CHOATE,	Woburn.
E. H. CHAMPNEY,	Woburn.
EBENEZER CLAPP,	Dorchester.
Rev. JAS. FREEMAN CLARKE,	Jamaica Plain.
GEO. W. CARNES,	Boston.
Hon. L. M. CRANE,	Dalton.
S. S. CURTIS,	Boston.
H. H. CHAMBERLIN,	Worcester.
Hon. OTIS CARY,	Foxborough.
FRANCIS CHILDS,	Boston.
JOHN CURTIS,	Boston.
Hon. J. E. CRANE,	Bridgewater.
Dr. BENJ. CUSHING,	Dorchester.
WM. E. COFFIN,	Dorchester.
Dr. WM. F. CHANNING,	Newport, R. I.
THOS. A. CAREW,	Cambridge.
WM. CHASE,	Salem.
CHAS. M. S. CHURCHILL,	Milton.
GEORGE COOLIDGE,	Boston.
DAVID CHAPIN,	Boston.
JOHN CUSHING,	South Hingham.
LABAN CUSHING,	South Hingham.
ANDREW CUSHING,	South Hingham.
Hon. CHAS. G. DAVIS,	Plymouth.
Hon. RICHARD H. DANA, Jr.,	Boston.
THOMAS DREW,	Boston.
J. D. DANIELS,	Worcester.
JOHN G. DWIGHT,	Boston.
JAS. H. DANFORTH,	Boston.
FREDERICK DOUGLASS,	Washington, D. C.
ANDREW W. DUNBAR,	South Hingham.

RALPH WALDO EMERSON,	Concord.
CHAS. M. ELLIS,	Boston.
WM. ENDICOTT, Jr.,	Boston.
Hon. M. M. FISHER,	Medway.
CHAS. FIELD,	Boston.
C. H. FITCH,	Worcester.
ABRAHAM FIRTH,	Boston.
JONAS FITCH,	Boston.
SAMUEL L. FEARING,	South Hingham.
CYRUS GALE,	Northborough.
Hon. D. W. GOOCH,	Boston.
PHINEAS GAY,	Boston.
HENRY GUILD,	Boston.
J. A. GIDDINGS,	Jefferson, Ohio.
Dr. ESTES HOWE,	Boston.
THOS. WENTWORTH HIGGINSON,	Newport, R. I.
JAS. G. HARTSHORNE,	Walpole.
Hon. E. R. HOAR,	Concord.
Hon. GEORGE F. HOAR,	Worcester.
JOSEPH K. HAYES,	Boston.
Rev. GILBERT HAVEN,	Boston.
Hon. MILO HILDRETH,	Northborough.
DEA. H. HUMPHREYS,	Dorchester.
FRANCIS HOWE,	Brookfield.
C. D. HARTSHORNE,	Walpole.
EDWARD HOLDEN,	Dorchester.
THOS. L. HARMAN,	Boston.
JOHN L. HAYES,	Boston.
LEWIS HAYDEN,	Boston.
AMASA HILAND,	Hingham Centre.
ALFRED A. HALL,	Boston.
Dr. EDWARD JARVIS,	Dorchester.
A. S. JORDAN,	Boston.
FRANKLIN KING,	Boston.
JOHN KNEELAND,	Dorchester.
ELIJAH E. KNOWLES,	Eastham.
M. P. KENNARD,	Boston.
H. A. LOTHROP,	Sharon.
Dr. O. MARTIN,	Worcester.
JOHN J. MAY,	Boston.
Hon. MARCUS MORTON,	Boston.
J. B. MANN,	Boston.
F. W. G. MAY,	Boston.
Hon. GEORGE H. MUNROE,	Boston.
GEORGE C. MANN,	Boston.
A. M. McPHAIL,	Boston.
Rev. A. D. MERRILL,	Boston.
JOSHUA MERRILL,	Boston.

WM. B. MERRILL, ... Boston.
HENRY A. MARSH, ... Worcester.
THOS. D. MORRIS, ... Boston.
Hon. S. C. MAINE, ... Boston.
CURTIS C. NICHOLS, . . . Boston.
FRED'K P. MOSELEY, . . . Boston.
JOHN A. NOWELL, ... Boston.
Rev. R. H. NEALE, D. D., . . Boston.
Hon. WILLARD P. PHILLIPS, . North Andover.
EDWARD L. PIERCE, . . . Boston.
Hon. HENRY L. PIERCE, . . Boston.
Hon. JOHN G. PALFREY, . . Cambridge.
Hon. CHAS. A. PHELPS, . . . Boston.
S. A. PORTER, ... Worcester.
WM. POPE, ... Boston.
JOSEPH PRATT, ... Worcester.
JOHN C. PARK, ... Boston.
EDWARD H. PAYSON, . . . Salem.
WENDELL PHILLIPS, . . . Boston.
Rev. A. P. PUTNAM, D. D., . . Brooklyn, N. Y.
JAMES T. ROBINSON, . . . North Adams.
Hon. THOMAS RUSSELL, . . Boston.
Hon. W. W. RICE, ... Worcester.
MARSHALL S. RICE, . . . Newton Centre.
SAMUEL B. RINDGE, . . . Boston.
GEORGE W. REED, ... Boston.
JOHN L. SWIFT, ... Boston.
CHAS. A. B. SHEPARD, . . . Boston.
CHAS. W. SLACK, ... Boston.
H. L. SABIN, ... Williamstown.
E. F. STONE, ... Newburyport.
S. E. SEWALL, ... Boston.
Hon. WM. B. SPOONER, . . Boston.
JAMES M. STONE, ... Boston.
Hon. CARL SCHURZ, . . . Washington.
HENRY C. SHEPARD, . . . Boston.
Gen. E. W. STONE, ... Boston.
OTIS SHEPARD, ... Boston.
GILBERT L. STREETER, . . Salem.
JOSEPH SARGENT, ... Boston.
J. B. SMITH, ... Boston.
ELIJAH SHUTE, ... South Hingham.
JOSEPH SPRAGUE, ... Hingham.
Hon. ADIN THAYER, . . . Worcester.
CALEB THAYER, ... Blackstone.
E. THOMPSON, ... East Walpole.
VELOROUS TAFT, ... Upton.

Rev. JAS. W. THOMPSON,	Jamaica Plain.
JOHN A. TUCKER,	Dorchester Lower Mills.
Dr. DAVID THAYER,	Boston.
WILDER S. THURSTON,	Lynn.
Hon. AMOS TUCK,	Exeter, N. H.
JOS. B. THAXTER,	Hingham.
JOHN WINSLOW,	New York.
JOSEPH WISWELL,	Milton.
THOS. C. WALES,	Boston.
CHAS. A. WOOD,	Boston.
EBEN WHEELWRIGHT,	Dorchester.
CALEB WALL,	Worcester.
Hon. WM. H. WOOD,	Middleborough.
Col. J. W. WETHERELL,	Worcester.
DAVID WHITON,	Hingham.
STARKES WHITON,	Hingham.
BELA H. WHITON,	Hingham Centre.
E. F. WATERS,	Boston.
GEORGE W. WATERS,	Newton Centre.
Prof. WEBSTER,	Wheaton, Ill.
J. M. W. YERRINTON,	Boston.
R. P. WATERS,	Beverly.
JOHN G. WHITTIER,	Danvers.
ELIZUR WRIGHT,	Boston.
Hon. OLIVER WARNER,	Arlington.
H. O. HILDRETH,	Dedham.
GEORGE F. WILLIAMS,	Boston.
FREEMAN WALKER,	North Brookfield.
E. B. STODDARD,	Worcester.
A. G. WALKER,	Worcester.
HARTLEY WILLIAMS,	Worcester.
J. W. ALDEN,	Cambridgeport.
Dr. LUTHER PARKS,	Boston.
Hon. ELI THAYER,	Worcester.
ALBERT TOLMAN,	Worcester.
W. H. FOX,	Taunton.
F. B. SANBORN,	Concord.
J. C. LINDSLEY,	Boston.
H. G. PARKER,	Boston.
WM. WITHINGTON,	Dorchester.
ABRAHAM PAYNE,	Providence, R. I.
GEORGE F. OSBORNE,	Boston.
STEPHEN C. WRIGHTINGTON,	Fall River.
NATHANIEL C. NASH,	Boston.
WILLARD SEARS,	Boston.
JAS. H. UPHAM,	Dorchester.

In response to this invitation, very many letters were received, some of which will be found in the Appendix. Most of them indicated the writer's acceptance of the invitation, and all expressed a hearty interest in the meeting, and sympathy with its objects and purposes.

On the day named, a large number of the guests left Boston on the steamer "Rose Standish," at half-past ten o'clock, and about an hour later, arrived at Downer Landing, where they were cordially met and welcomed by Mr. Downer, Edmands' Band, which was stationed on the wharf, playing "Auld Lang Syne." A procession was formed, headed by the Hon. Charles Francis Adams and Mr. Downer, which, preceded by the band, marched to the garden, where the time, until the arrival of the noon boat, was delightfully spent in the renewal of old acquaintanceships, in reminiscences of the many stirring events of the old days of slavery domination, and in rambling over the beautiful grounds, which nature has made so attractive, and to which art and taste have given additional charms.

Soon after one o'clock, the steamer "John Romer" arrived with many other guests, who were received in the same manner as their predecessors. When they reached the garden, a procession was formed, embracing nearly two hundred gentlemen, who, escorted by the band, marched to the pavilion, where a bountiful fish dinner was served. Mr. Downer presided at the table. On his right sat Hon. Charles Francis Adams of Quincy, Hon. Wm. Claflin of Newton, Hon. Charles G. Davis of Plymouth, Hon. Geo. F. Hoar and Hon. Adin Thayer of Worcester, Hon. Wm. B. Spooner and Rev. Rollin H. Neale of Boston. On his left sat Hon. John B. Alley of Lynn, Hon. Francis W. Bird of East Walpole, Rev. James Freeman Clarke of Boston, Hon. E. Rockwood Hoar of Concord, M. P. Kennard, Esq., of Brookline, Hon. Willard P. Phillips of North Andover, and Hon.

Amos Tuck of Exeter, N. H. The Divine blessing was invoked by the Rev. James Freeman Clarke, as follows :—

O thou Infinite Spirit of Justice and Truth, we bless thee for this hour, when those who, through long years of struggle for the same great principles of right, are allowed to look into each others' faces now, and bless thee for the triumph of thine eternal justice here below. We bless thee, Heavenly Father, that thou hast taught us by thy providence that thy truths are mighty and will prevail, and that there is a providence ruling in the affairs of men, and that throughout this great land, no foot which is not free shall ever press its soil again, and that every man here shall have the right to sit under his own tree, and by his own fire, and bless thee for equal and impartial rights. And now, we ask nothing for ourselves, for thou hast given us all in permitting us to see this great triumph of that which we loved better than ourselves; but we ask that this land of our love may be evermore animated by these great principles of justice and right, and that, in this country, no race shall ever be trampled upon, and no class ever put down by unequal laws, but that all shall be equal and free forever before thee; which we ask in the name of thy divine mercy and thy perfect justice. Amen.

Mr. DOWNER. We all very well know that soldiers, whether engaged in a good or a bad cause, always fight best on full stomachs. That rule will hold good with regard to Free-Soilers, who always fight in a good cause; therefore, let us fill the inner man, and then we shall be ready to listen to our friends, who, we know, will speak the right word in the right place.

After an hour very agreeably spent in disposing of the many good things with which the tables were loaded, the assembly was called to order by Mr. DOWNER, who said: I was once in Faneuil Hall when the meeting was about to be addressed by that grand old man, now passed away, JOSIAH QUINCY, Sr. On rising to speak, he said that, fearing to rely on his memory, he had brought his speech in his pocket, and I thought I could not do better than copy such an illustrious example.

Mr. Downer then read the following—

ADDRESS OF WELCOME.

My Friends and Fellow Free-Soilers of 1848:

I bid you a most heartfelt and fervent welcome. I feel, as I also believe you feel, that those of us who, either as members at the primary meetings, as delegates to the Buffalo Convention, or who early acted with the party, and who remained faithful to the movement till 1856, need no other bond to make us welcome this meeting than to know we were of them. With your permission, I wish to make a few preliminary remarks, and will then yield the chair to one whom it will give you more pleasure to listen to than to me. And here let me observe, this company was invited to meet with the sole object of indulging in pleasant reminiscences of the past; for I know when Free-Soilers meet twenty-nine years after the formation of the party at Buffalo, when we recollect how fervent and united we were, it cannot be other than cheerful and happy. It is intended to be informal, and we anticipate listening to those who, twenty-nine years ago, stirred up the fires of freedom, when it required some courage and backbone to do so. To-day we are met to congratulate ourselves that we, living, again clasp each other's hands in kindly recollection of those days; and to-day we are met to call up our tender sympathies in memory of the departed great, who, if in God's providence it is permitted them to look down upon us, we know are with us here in sympathy also.

My friends, it is the custom, when one is about to address a meeting, to speak humbly of one's self; but as I stand here, I cannot, for the life of me, avoid appearing egotistical.

A few months ago, when our country was in fear and alarm, growing out of the uncertainty of the Presidential election, I happened into the office of Mr. Edward L. Pierce, the biographer of our lamented Sumner. I said to him: As I meet our old Free-Soilers in the street, their patriotism is as fervent as ever; but they hold all kinds of opinions, and I wish we could meet again and light up those old fires to cheer and comfort us. He said it was an excellent idea. I afterward spoke of it to my old friend, Frank W. Bird. The result was this meeting. And now, when I look upon these upturned faces, glowing with the spirit of 1848, desiring now as then to know where true patriotism is pointing and to follow,—when I feel we shall hear voices telling us what they think, and warming us with the old fires,—I cannot help saying I am a pretty cute Yankee to have made for myself the privilege of opening this meeting. But, gentlemen, though I hold the position, don't be alarmed, I will not keep it long. I know myself too well for that, and, besides, I have another cause for self-elation. When I wrote the resolution at the primary meeting in Old Dorchester, which was to choose delegates to the Buffalo Convention, I tried my hand at prophecy. I must read one to show whether I was a good prophet or not:—

Resolved, That we return our heartfelt thanks to those true patriots, Judge Charles Allen and the Hon. Henry Wilson, and those of the Ohio and Indiana delegations to the late convention at Philadelphia, who, when Freedom's voice was drowned and her spirit crushed,— who, when so many were silent, or worse than silent,—resolutely spurned the bribe. We believe the time will come, when both at the North and at the South, at the East and at the West, their names will be honored and remembered, when those who now censure and revile them will have sunk into oblivion.

My friends, I want to recall reminiscences of two who were of note in those times. I do it as an example to others to do likewise. As I stand now, I see plainly, as if a reality, Daniel Webster. He was the god of my political idolatry. Ah! how fervently have I listened to his grand constitutional arguments! How I have burned at the words of freedom he spoke for man! When our

Free-Soil party was first started, we thought he was with us. There are those of us who know that when the late lamented Stephen C. Phillips penned the opening address to be delivered at Faneuil Hall, Webster revised it, and interlined what he thought was more appropriate. Alas! alas! that was his last effort for human freedom! We know that evening he went to New York, instead of coming down to Faneuil Hall; we know how his friends at Buffalo sought his nomination to the Presidency,—not on new pledges, but from his known past record. After the nomination of Van Buren and Adams, how bitter he was to us, to Van Buren, and to Taylor! We know it all culminated in his 7th of March speech of 1850; and we know the South, which he courted so hard, begrudged him even a poor complimentary vote. My friends, if Daniel Webster erred against the record of his life and the convictions of his conscience, grievously did he pay the penalty. Let us draw the veil over that portion of his life. Oh! that he had died a few years sooner, or had lived a few years longer! The first gun at Sumter would have set him right. He was my teacher, and from him I learned the principles of constitutional liberty. Peace to his ashes!

I have but one other name to mention, and then I will close,—Horace Mann. It was my happy lot to know him intimately—most intimately. He was the most self-sacrificing man I ever knew. Forty years ago I resided in the same house with him, and our rooms were adjoining. It was at the commencement of his educational movement. How well I remember his intense labors, extending into the early hours of the morning, and the vast correspondence he maintained! This he endured for twelve years without complaint, and it was only when his successor was to be appointed, that he told the Legislature that an office and a clerk were needed, and they were readily granted. When the mantle of the "old man eloquent" fell upon him by the spontaneous wish of the people, I remember the remark he made to me. He said: "I shall soon issue my twelfth annual report to the board of education. I think I have laid the foundation of the educational movement that has been so dear to me, and I think if I give place to others, they now can do more than I can in carrying out my plans. I think, if I accept this nomination, I may do some good in the causes of education, temperance, and anti-slavery, and whenever I can strike a blow for either of them, I will do it; but my aspirations for political life are over. I shall never again be a party man in a political sense." We know the result; he was almost unanimously chosen. He did not enter often into debate, but when he did speak, how effective it was! He was much consulted by all parties, and many were the anecdotes he told me of conversations with the then fire-eating Southerners. His election to the second term was made under very different circumstances. Webster's 7th of March speech struck a deep and painful wound, and it was yet fresh. How hard and how successfully he combated it! The old Whig element of the State was arrayed against him. You all remember his taking the stump, planting himself on the broad ground, "I have only done what I promised to do,—to strike a blow against slavery whenever it should array itself against freedom!" You know of his triumphant re-election. Before the expiration of his term, he was nominated as governor of Massachusetts, but the Free-Soil element had not then got into the ascendant. Before the next election, he had received an invitation to become the president of Antioch College, where he remained until his death. The college was not what it had been represented to him. It was in debt, with its means of support already exhausted in investments; in fact, I think its foundation was in a land speculation. He said to me, consulting me: "I have seen much of the West; they are young and vigorous, and will hereafter play *the* important part in the destinies of our country. I find the young are inclined to scepticism in religion, and the old to bigotry. The Christian sect has planted itself on the Bible as the foundation, the interpretation of which is left to each one's individual mind. I can stand on that, and I hope I can give broader and higher views than now exist." You know he entered on Sundays the pulpit, and had large congregations from all the country around. During the whole of his remaining life, he struggled with their poverty and with their little dissensions. At the time of his death, the college had been sold, and passed into Unitarian hands, and was out of debt, but still poor. His constitution had become enfeebled, and his person much emaciated by hard and continual work, and he gradually sunk under it; but he continued his labors to the very end. I do not think he knew how worn his system was. On the day he died, his physician told him he had but a very few hours to live. It struck him with much surprise, and he questioned him closely. When convinced it was so, he said, "Then I have no time to lose," and calling a few of the remaining students—for it was vacation time—and his family around him, he gave them wise counsel, to be true to their highest conviction, and to rely on a just God. He even went so far as to point out to students their individual temptations. When he got through, he said he was fatigued, and would rest. And thus passed from earth Horace Mann. He had an intuitive intellect, which almost amounted to inspiration. He was an intense, hard worker, and many were the good works for the prisoner, the insane, and the ignorant, that he accomplished. And in the familiar intercourse with those he loved, with his wit, his humor, his acquirements, and his ever out-cropping benevolence, oh, how dear he became to us! His life was a useful one, and his end a triumphant and happy one.

My friends, I have made these few remarks on two

individuals whose lives stamped themselves deep in my memory. I hope that by those who follow me the strong impressions left on them by our departed Free-Soil great men may be given to us; that our meeting may be a cheerful and happy one. And let it be remembered, that after the lapse of twenty-nine years from our convention, the slave is free, and to-day the great interest of us all is to have one country, and a firm and happy Union. I care not how it comes. Carpet-bagism is buried in the grave that knows no resurrection. Whether it comes from the rejuvenated Republican party or the Democratic party, or the cream of both acting together, *God speed its coming!* I now have the great pleasure of calling to the chair I perhaps have occupied too long, one who has consented to serve us, and whose life is stamped in living characters,— the Hon. Charles Francis Adams.

ADDRESS OF THE HON. CHARLES FRANCIS ADAMS.

Gentlemen:—Our friend, Mr. Downer, has been pleased to summon us to this, his magnificent seat of repose, on a day which he has himself selected as being an anniversary of a most interesting event in our political history. On the 9th of August, 1848, an assembly of delegates from a large number of the free States of our Union was held at Buffalo, in the State of New York, to consider the question, What might be done, on the approach of the election, then about to be held, of a new President and Vice-President, to change the current of the national policy, which had been long setting in the direction of a permanent establishment of the institution of human slavery as an overruling power in the State forever and aye. Our worthy host has been pleased to call upon me to preside on this occasion, for no reason I can imagine except that it happened to me to have been called to the same duty on that occasion, twenty-nine years ago. At that time he and I were entitled still to be counted among the working members of society. But now that we both are on the verge prescribed in Scripture as closing all worldly enjoyments, I am led to conclude that he gathers us around him as a last chance for a good friendly talk, once more to fight our battles over again. [Applause.] Permit me, then, to remind you, as briefly as possible, what was the state of the country prior to the time when the demonstration at Buffalo was made. From the close of the short war with Great Britain, in 1815, to the year 1821, but a single question of serious importance had agitated the people. That question was connected with the admission of the Territory of Missouri into the Union, and involved the right of Congress to annex a condition to it of excluding the institution of negro slavery from its borders. This was the first great battle for liberty, and it ended in what went by the name of the Missouri compromise, or, in clearer terms, a bargain that was not a settlement. Twenty years passed away, and it began to be apparent that the extension of the political power favored by the Missouri decision had become a ruling principle among the slaveholders, and the entire policy of the country had been gradually made to bend to the establishment of an idol stronger than the old image of liberty,—the grim idol of slavery, threatening to spread its baleful influence over indefinite millions of human beings yet unborn. The first indications of dissatisfaction with this prospect of the future did not make their appearance among the more active and prominent statesmen of the time. Content with the position they had gained by their public services, they were not disposed to shake it by countenancing startling problems. It was reserved for a wholly different class of the community to enter upon this formidable enterprise of bearding the lion in his den. Standing as we do now, independent and impartial judges of the past, I am free to say that we owe a great debt of gratitude to that small band of courageous men, and women too, who, having no fear of obloquy before them, and yet conscious of the danger that might beset them from their adoption of a most unpopular cause, went on boldly, in the face of a malignant and dangerous opposition, to uphold with steady perseverance the cause of justice, of humanity, and of truth. [Applause.] Many of the heroes and heroines of that day have passed away from among us and entered upon their reward. But a few still remain to enjoy the proud satisfaction of a faithful performance of a hazardous duty, recognized by the joint acclamations of all later generations of mankind.

But I must hasten with my story.

For a time the slave power went on, apparently having its own way without opposition. State after State was marked out and admitted to the Union from the territory already acquired, recognizing slavery, until it was exhausted, yet the power did not quite keep up with the corresponding progress of the free States. It was then that the plan was devised of acquiring the vast regions exclusively in the South and West, in which it might be practicable to spread the hateful policy indefinitely. Beginning with the accession of General Jackson to power, it went on steadily, whenever opportunity offered to the leaders to gain their points, either fairly, or when not fairly, by force or fraud. At last the community began to grow slowly conscious that matters were going wrong. Florida had been fairly bought, but Texas had been stolen from the Mexicans through the expedient of pretended colonization. The next step was to pick a quarrel with Mexico. In order to bring this about, it became necessary to carry an election of a proper agent to the Presidency. To that end it was not deemed prudent to bring forward any well-known leader for a slaveholding candidate. The managers finally pitched upon James K. Polk, a respectable gentleman from

Tennessee, once speaker of the house, but so little known that the story went about, that when the news of his nomination came to the ears of the assemblies of the faithful in the North, they first bravely cheered James K. Polk, and next shouted the question, Who was James K. Polk?

Against this feeble nomination the Whigs presented the name of Henry Clay, a man so well known to everybody for his long and brilliant public services, that his party, in comparing his name with that of Polk, scoffed at the possibility of failing to elect their favorite. Yet, when the election came round, lo and behold, James K. Polk was chosen! You may ask what was the reason of this singular change. It was all because of a letter written by Mr. Clay, giving his views of the proposal to annex Texas, which he wrote so equivocally, that, when it came to be known in Western New York, it alienated from him just about votes enough to turn the scale in that State against him, and that turned the scale again in the electoral vote of the whole country. The slaveholders triumphed, and the victors set about at once to secure the profits of the victory. Not satisfied with Texas only, their next step was to pick a quarrel with Mexico, because she did not approve that sort of stealing. This was so skilfully managed as to involve an ultimate appeal to war. Of all the flagitious schemes of the slaveholders to extend their power over new territory, no one has ever seemed to me so utterly indefensible as this. As one of many zealous friends of the cause of freedom, I had worked my full share in behalf of Mr. Clay and the Whigs, notwithstanding his equivocal letter. And when we saw the atrocity of the method now adopted by the slave party to extend the limits of their victory, we fully expected that it would be met with a corresponding unflinching resistance by the united efforts of all their opponents. You may judge of our surprise, when we found that there was no intention in the party to regard these questions as a party at all. Every member was to vote as he thought best. Some of them actually voted for the war. From that instant my own attachment to this organization became so weakened, that I decided to decline any further the trust which had been liberally extended to me in the Massachusetts Legislature for several years. Neither was I alone in holding these sentiments. As the policy of the slaveholders went on, many persons of great weight of character seemed more and more satisfied with the utter indifference manifested by the Whigs. The tone of their newspapers was absolutely servile, and the spirit of opposition became completely hushed. A few of us, after consultation together, decided that we could not continue silent in this emergency. The chief difficulty was in finding any political organ that would express our sentiments as freely as we desired. Just at that moment it so happened that a newspaper press which had been started in the height of the late election, made known to me first as edited by a son of Joseph T. Buckingham of the "Courier," well remembered by many of us here, and which had lost all chance of establishing itself after the loss of the election, in pure desperation was offered to me by the printers who controlled it. The paper bore the name of the "Boston Whig." After some conversation respecting the details, I was so far tempted by this opportunity offered to the knot of friends who sympathized with me in maintaining the ground we had taken against the backsliding of our party, as to call them together and lay the matter fully before them. The result was that a meeting was called at "Lobby No. 13," in the State House, by John G. Palfrey, then Secretary of the Commonwealth [applause], to which had been invited by me Stephen C. Phillips of Salem [applause], Charles Sumner of Boston [applause], and Henry Wilson of Natick [applause]. These three, and Dr. Palfrey and myself, constituted the little company. After much discussion and a variety of opinions, it was ultimately decided to accept the offer made to us, and to enter on the experiment. To that a contribution of money was to be made. Dr. Palfrey agreed to assume the responsibility for one-fifth of the sum required, Mr. Phillips and I, respectively, took two-fifths, while the other two gentlemen, less favored by fortune, pledged themselves to make up for the difference in earnest and vigorous support of the undertaking, and that they faithfully gave.

Such was the beginning of the Republican party in the State of Massachusetts. Of all the men engaged in this primitive undertaking, desperate as it seemed, no single one contributed more to its success than John G. Palfrey. [Applause.] Apart from his pecuniary assistance, which was large in its proportion to his means, he began the campaign with that very able series of papers on the slave power, which were afterwards collected and circulated, producing a great effect on opinion wherever they went. [At this point Mr. F. W. Bird rose and said: "Dr. Palfrey is physically unable to be here to-day. I ask the audience to rise and give three cheers for that venerable and honored man." The audience rose and gave three hearty cheers.] No more sterling patriot and statesman is to be found in the long list of our public men. He still survives, the only one, except myself, of a company all of whom put in their strength to bring about the great revolution that has since taken place in our land. It is no more than just that posterity should retain the memory of their names forever.

It becomes me to add another name,—that of one who sympathized with us entirely in our undertaking, and who did marvels in promoting it at the very start. Need I mention the name of Charles Allen [applause], whose eloquent appeal to the people of Worcester County, of whom he was the chosen representative, laid a permanent foundation in that region in favor of freedom that has remained solid down to this day?

But the time warns me that I must be brief. We fought the battle of freedom in the "Whig" with various fortune, until the time came for a new election to the Presidency. The question then came up, What should we do? We had not separated from the Whig party, nor did we mean to separate unless we should clearly see that the principles professed by all in common were to be deliberately abandoned on occasions by the greater number. The nominations of the respective parties were about to be made. The administration of President Polk had ended by a triumphant war, attended by an enormous accretion of new territory for the benefit of slavery. Of that war, General Taylor had been the successful guide; hence his popularity had grown in proportion. Yet the fact was indisputable, that he was a citizen of a slave State, and a proprietor of large estates on which he kept large numbers of negroes in slavery. How, then, could he be made acceptable to any true friends of freedom? On the other hand, the Democratic party, responsible for the making of the war, and pledged to a policy favoring the extension of slavery in the territory acquired by it, brought forward General Lewis Cass as a faithful exponent of their established policy. In this emergency, what was our consternation when we found that the Whig opponent of General Cass was to be General Taylor, the man of all others who had by his victories done the most of all to uphold the administration,—a large slaveholder, pledged by his property and his negro laborers to protect, if not to extend, the odious system which we had so fiercely denounced. In this dilemma, the painful question arose, What was to be done to maintain our consistency? To vote for Lewis Cass would be giving a sanction to the policy of the war, which we abhorred. To vote for General Taylor would be glorifying the agent who had done so much to promote results which we held in dread. There was one alternative, and that was a resort to a third nomination. It could not hope to be successful, or to be more than a solemn protest against the tendency of both parties. Yet, after a careful survey of the ground, there seemed to be reasonable cause for believing that our action, whatever it might be, would have no small effect in consolidating a party that might overcome resistance in time, if not then. The only question of difficulty, was whom we should nominate as our candidate. On the one side there had been a considerable secession in the State of New York from the Democratic nomination of General Cass. On the other there was an almost equal disgust among the Whig moderate men at the nomination of General Taylor, and this feeling pointed very distinctly to the substitution of Judge John McLean of Ohio.

For one I must acknowledge that I was much exercised at the time by the unfortunate turn that these elections had taken. To vote for General Taylor was flying in the face of the principles we had solemnly put forward. A resort to General Cass was equally out of the question. How it might be with Mr. Van Buren, we could not tell. In any event, it seemed indispensable to take steps to assemble another convention. A very considerable number of persons of influence gave in favorable responses to the proposition, and the requisite steps were taken to carry it into effect. Buffalo, in New York, was fixed upon as the place, and the ninth day of August the time, for the assembling of this new combination. Many people, particularly in the State of Massachusetts, had been much roused by the events which had taken place; and, as a consequence, a full delegation was sent to Buffalo, embracing many of the most promising young men growing up in the State. In the district in which I lived, the meeting was pleased to name me as one of the delegates, and I cheerfully obeyed the call. In a few days I found myself in the midst of the multitude assembled for that great meeting. There have been many such assemblages since, far larger in numbers, and perhaps more skilful in their modes of operation, but for plain, downright honesty of purpose to effect high ends without a whisper of bargain and sale, I doubt whether any similar one has been its superior, either before or since. [Applause.] The first duty after our arrival was to consult with our brethren of other States, respecting the selection of a candidate to represent our views, as opposed to those entertained by both the older parties. I soon discovered that a nomination would certainly be made, and the selection of the man would be narrowed down between Judge McLean and Martin Van Buren, one a Whig, the other a Democrat. The question was which of the two was to be preferred. His party character was of little consequence. I think I have already said that my own inclinations tended to the preference of Judge McLean, and to that end I applied at once to the delegates from Ohio for concerted action in his behalf. The chief person in that highly respectable delegation was Mr. S. P. Chase [applause], a promising statesman, whose later career is familiar to you all; and to him I was referred for authentic information of Judge McLean's position. You may judge of my surprise, when I was informed that the judge was severely tried,—wavering on the anxious seat,—with strong aversion to be pitted against any rival candidate. The effect of this wet blanket over our hopes you can readily imagine.

For some such emergency as now presented itself I had not been altogether unprepared. In the event of the retreat of Judge McLean, it was obvious that the friends of Mr. Van Buren would necessarily, by their union and organization, have the advantage over any other public man whom we could persuade to stand, and these we could count on our fingers' ends. Not entirely blind to this possibility, I had already, in my private capacity, taken a step on my own responsibility, to open the way for this possible alternative. On the 16th of July,—that is, three weeks previous,—I had addressed a confidential letter to Mr. Van Buren, reciting the nature of our movement, and the encouraging symptoms in his Presidential career adverse to the Texas policy, and calling upon him to give me such an explicit answer as I might have it in my power to use in his favor in case of an emergency, which I apprehended might take place. Martin Van Buren has long since passed away, and his confidential letter in answer to mine can never do him any harm, if it should now pass into the province of American history.

Here it is, and I will read it to you:—

[CONFIDENTIAL.] LINDENWALD, July 24, 1848.

MY DEAR SIR:—I have received your letter, and although you do not desire an answer, I cannot in justice to my own feelings refrain from expressing the satisfaction I have derived from its good sense, liberal and manly spirit.

It has afforded me much pleasure to find that you at least understand what it is so difficult to make most people comprehend,—"the involuntary character of the relation which I occupy to the public." So far was I from desiring to be a candidate for the Presidency, that it would have required other and stronger considerations than those which were then presented to me to have prevented me from declining the office itself, if those who asked me to be a candidate had possessed the power of placing it at my disposal. When the letter which is in part the subject of your approbation, and, in all, of fair criticism, was written, nothing could have been farther from my mind than that it would be considered by the public in connection with my present position. You will see by the terms of the letter addressed to me by the New York delegation, that they were well apprised of the character of my resolution upon one of the points of their address. All that they had a right to expect was an unreserved expression of my opinions upon the other questions they presented, and this I gave them with pleasure. The most prominent men in the convention, who were sincerely desirous of respecting my known wishes, lost the control of its movements in regard to the nomination after the reading of my letter, and the result is known to all. Although brought before the country in this unexpected and extraordinary manner, it did not require much reflection to satisfy me that the course I have adopted was the only one that was open to me, and to that I will, of course, adhere. This matter will be found more fully noticed in a letter from me to the industrial congress recently assembled at Philadelphia, which will appear in the "Evening Post" of to-morrow. In that I have also set forth, after full consideration, the course I design to pursue in regard to any further expositions of my views upon public questions. My reasons for adopting it are given as fully as the limits of such a document would permit. They will, I hope, be satisfactory to many, but, whether they are or not, I shall feel myself, constrained to adhere to the position I have taken.

It can, under existing circumstances, be scarcely necessary to say, that if any of your friends think they can give more effect to their principles upon the main subject, by taking a course different from that to which your own feelings seem inclined, or if it would for any reasons be more agreeable to them to do so, their conduct in the matter will not be disagreeable to me in any sense. My solicitude has been, not to get nominations, but to keep clear of them, and nothing can be done at Buffalo that is founded on good sense, and looks in good faith to the advancement of the great principle I hold sacred, which will cause me either regret or mortification.

I have marked this letter confidential, because I have received a vast number of communications upon the same subject, which I am compelled to leave unanswered, as I have done, I believe, in every case except yours, and I desire to avoid giving offence as far as I can. The views it takes I do not hesitate to express to all who desire to understand them. Whilst, therefore, reasonable caution is observed in regard to the fact of our correspondence, I shall be content that you speak of my opinions and dispositions as you now understand them.

I am very respectfully and truly yours,

M. VAN BUREN.

CHARLES FRANCIS ADAMS, ESQ.

This letter had been received on the 20th of July. Although somewhat wordy, it substantially ratified and confirmed his former declarations and his policy, which practically cost him the Democratic nomination. That went to General Cass. There was then nothing left to us to choose, but to raise up Martin Van Buren as the most courageous man of high position in the two parties willing then to hold up our standard. His clear answer to the invitation sealed the bond, and from the 19th of August,

1848, the great party dates the organization which, through weal and through woe, at last carried to a triumphant close a struggle for a mighty principle which, for its length and severity, is entitled to claim a high and honorable rank in the annals of the world.

As for Massachusetts, you all doubtless remember the result of that election, which forced an entering-wedge into the Whig column that ultimately effected its downfall. In contrast with this struggle all later questions sink into insignificance. Let us rejoice that we now live in the full enjoyment of all the blessings that attend good government,—peace, freedom, and justice, environed by plenty and supported by law.

I have, I fear, Mr. Downer, intrenched much too far on the festivities of this occasion and deprived your guests of the privilege of hearing the experience of others whom I see around me, all of them more or less associated with the event you have been pleased to celebrate to-day.

Gentlemen, during the period in which I had the honor to serve our State, there occurred an event of great interest, in which it happened to be my fate to be somewhat engaged. I do not know why it was, but somehow or other, whenever any question about slavery came up in the General Court, in either branch, it seemed to be the disposition of the Speaker to send it to me, on a committee. Under these circumstances, I had a great many questions presented; but one of the most serious ones was in connection with a law of South Carolina, which prescribed that when any negro should arrive in any port of that State, no matter in what vessel he was, he should be taken at once to prison, and kept there during the whole time the vessel remained in port. There was so much dissatisfaction created by that law, both in England and here, that it was made the subject of remonstrance, and accordingly a petition was sent to the General Court, requesting that some measures might be taken in order, if possible, to protect those men. As usual, that petition was referred to me, as the chairman of a committee, and it was my fate, or my good fortune, to be able to make a report, the substance of which was a request to the Governor to take the necessary measures to communicate to the State of South Carolina the dissatisfaction of Massachusetts with this law. We therefore obtained from the Legislature authority for him to send an agent to South Carolina for that purpose. I need not tell you, gentlemen, that that agent was Mr. SAMUEL HOAR, and how he was treated in his mission. [Loud applause.] He has gone from us, but he has left behind him two distinguished gentlemen whom I have in my eye, who have each in turn done great service to the cause and to the country. [Renewed applause.] I therefore call upon the elder of those gentlemen to say a word on this occasion. [Applause.]

ADDRESS OF THE HON. E. ROCKWOOD HOAR.

MR. CHAIRMAN, FRIENDS:—A very estimable lady, to whom I was once introduced in Washington, asked me if Mr. Hoar, of the House of Representatives, was not my brother, and I admitted he was. Said she, "He is considerably older than you, isn't he?" I told her there was a difference of ten years between us. She looked at me a moment, and said she supposed he was older, but had no idea it was so much. And as he is in public life and I am not, I should much have preferred, Mr. Chairman, that whatever might have fallen to the lot of our family in the way of speech-making, should have been conferred upon him.

I have imitated our excellent host and yourself, sir, by bringing no other speech here than what I have in my pocket, and I don't know that I ever experienced so much satisfaction in finding my pocket empty. I am very much obliged to Mr. Downer for the privilege of being here, and on looking around at this assembly, bringing back the memory of almost or quite thirty years, and looking up at these rafters, I can almost imagine that I see here, not exactly hung up, because they are down on the floor, what is left of the seed-corn of that generation. I believe that the men here assembled exercised that function as much as any body of men that could now be assembled,— the seed-corn from which the crop has come which we have all witnessed. I think it is pleasant to go back into those days of memory. You have very fully gone over them, sir, and as I have no speech to make, I will not take up the time of this company with any attempt to follow in your footsteps.

I remember those who are gone of the faithful and able men who were among our leaders and our brethren in that cause, and I am happy, sir, I believe for the first time in my life, in paying a humble tribute to the late Mr. Van Buren. Our support of him personally in that contest of 1848 was not enthusiastic, and the thing I remember most distinctly about it was an observation made just after the nomination at the Buffalo Convention by an old farmer from the western part of the State of New York, who was a member of the convention, who had been trained as a Whig, and to whom, as to me, the associations with Mr. Van Buren were by no means fragrant. He was sorely disappointed at the nomination, but concluded to support it, as we all did eventually, uncaring for the consequences. "Well," said he, "I suppose we shall have to take him, and I shall support him; and there is one good thing about him; I always understood that he stuck strong to his side and to whatever he went for, for the time being. I remember that when he said 'the spiles to the victors,' the victors had 'em."

THE PRESIDENT. I regret very much that I am deprived of the opportunity of calling upon the brother of our friend who has just sat down, as I should probably have done, for the reason that he has requested me not to call on him. [Cries of "Call him out," "Hoar."] I think, gentlemen, the only authority which would be likely to operate upon him would come from you, yourselves. [Applause.]

Three cheers were then given for Senator Hoar, and the President added, "I think it is impossible, under these circumstances, that he can refuse you."

ADDRESS OF THE HON. GEORGE F. HOAR.

MR. PRESIDENT:—I requested you not to call upon me on this occasion for two very satisfactory reasons. The first is, that I have been laboring under a very troublesome abscess in one of my ears, which so oppresses that as to deprive me of the sense of hearing on one side, and so oppresses my brain that if I were to attempt to make a speech, you would desire to be deprived of the sense of hearing on both sides before I got through. [Laughter.] The other reason was this: That the people of Worcester, emulating the habit of their associates and predecessors in the Free-Soil movement of 1848, undertook to make among themselves some arrangements suited for this occasion, before communicating them to the outside world, and we agreed that no man should be permitted to make a speech here to-day, or be called upon, who could not show his title to the respect of the audience, by proving that he had made one in the year 1848, and I am not quite old enough to come within that excellent rule. My relation to the Free-Soil party of 1848—being then a law student, just out of college, and just past my twenty-first birthday—was that of folding the circulars written by my elder brother [laughter], and helping direct them, which invited the assemblage of the meeting on the twenty-eighth day of June in that year,—the State Convention at Worcester,—from which the convention at Buffalo, whose history in such an interesting manner has been related by the Chairman, sprung. The meeting was held on the Common, in Worcester. I was at that time a boy in the full flush of youthful hope and expectation, having studied, as other New England boys had studied, the lives of our Revolutionary fathers, and the history of the great battles which liberty had won in the past. I had the privilege of attending that meeting, as did many gentlemen into whose faces I am now looking; and it was a scene which few persons who witnessed it will ever be likely to forget,— made interesting from the sublimity of the step which its members were about to take; made interesting for its great consequences in the freedom of the race; made interesting for the subsequent distinction and influence in our political history of the gentlemen who made it up, and who managed it.

The prominent person in that meeting has already been alluded to by the Chairman,—a gentleman who, it seems to me, I exaggerate nothing in saying, was the superior in intellectual force to any man who has lived within the limits of the Commonwealth in my time. I allude to Charles Allen. [Great applause.] He was a man of slender frame, unequal to great physical labor, of delicate voice, capable only of addressing silent and listening audiences; but yet, in the sagacity which selected a position, whether at the bar or in political life, and in the intellectual power which defended it against all antagonists, it seems to me he never had a superior or an equal in this Commonwealth, within the memory of the present generation. [Applause.]

Judge Allen had been the delegate of the people of the Worcester district, then constituting, with the Genesee district in New York and the Lancaster district in Pennsylvania, the three strongest Whig districts in the country. He had attended that convention at Philadelphia, when the Whig party, after a long absence from political power, seemed just about to grasp the administration of the country, and under the prestige of General Taylor's popularity, to compromise itself by doing an injustice and a wrong as the price of a long lease of power and authority in the country. And in that convention, that slender, quiet man, with his feeble voice, had the hardihood to rise in the midst of that excited and exultant assemblage and pronounce that the Whig party was dissolved. [Great applause.]

But with the exception of his personal knowledge of the temper of the city and county which he himself represented, I suppose Judge Allen could not have given a good reason for supposing that in that declaration he should have the support of a dozen villages throughout the length and breadth of this land. Both parties—all the prominent statesmen, all the forces of national and state governments throughout these thirty States—were pledged to the support of slavery, or to a refusal, at any rate, to interfere with its progress; and yet Judge Allen presented the sublime spectacle of coming home from Philadelphia to appeal to the people of the United States to make good that prophecy.

There is another reminiscence of that time, which I may perhaps be pardoned in alluding to, somewhat to the credit of my own native town of Concord. The people of that little town—the natives—have been sometimes charged with an overweening sense of its importance, and vanity in regard to its excellence. I am not one of those individuals who share that opinion. I think, taking the town of Concord on one side and the rest of the world on the other, on the whole, there is quite, or at any rate nearly, as much excellence in the other part of the world as there is in the town of Concord. [Laughter.] But however that may be, it happened that the first three great public meetings which were held to indorse the action of Charles Allen and Henry Wilson, and to found a new party on the principles which they had announced when they bolted from the Philadelphia Convention, were presided over by natives of that town,—one in Lowell, by our genial and lamented friend, whose writings have passed into the political literature of the country, the late William S. Robinson [applause]; another, the meeting on the 28th of June, on the Common, at Worcester, presided over by Samuel Hoar; and the other, a vast meeting held in the City Hall, at Worcester, to receive Judge Allen on his return, presided over by our honored and excellent friend, Mr. Albert Tolman, who now does me the honor to listen to me. That meeting was held on the 15th of June, preliminary to the great State convention on the 28th. At that State convention assembled a very remarkable company of men. There, on the platform, was our distinguished President of to-day, uttering by inherited right the famous sentence: "Sink or swim, live or die, survive or perish, I give my heart and my hand to this movement" [applause], and, as was well said by a speaker who followed, "with the voice of the Revolution upon his lips." There was the manly form of Charles Sumner [applause], in the splendor and vigor and magnetic power of his youthful eloquence,—a power which he never, it seemed to me, fully recovered after the assault upon him in the Senate Chamber by Preston Brooks. There, too, was the noble head of Charles Allen, with its exquisite lines [applause], comely as was ever carved in cameo by Italian artist on costliest stone or shell. Others whom we should be glad to remember on this day were there. There was Erastus Hopkins [applause], a man of intellectual vigor and eloquence, probably surpassed by none of the gentlemen engaged in that movement in the power of stirring and stimulating a crowded audience by public speech,—a gentleman now well represented in this Commonwealth by his accomplished and promising son. There, too, was Stephen C. Phillips, whose name is well represented here to-day. [Applause.]

And what a lesson, my friends, has been the result of that little meeting, which assembled amid the jeers and the sneers and the scoffs of a hostile press and an incredulous people, in showing that, in political movements, a reliance on simple justice, on the simple law of equality, on simple truth, never will fail in human history, and never will fail of support by the American people! [Applause.] The Whig leaders of that day, the Democratic leaders of that day, the men who opposed this little movement, with its twenty or thirty thousand people in Massachusetts alone in the country behind it, have gone, almost all of them, to forgotten graves. The history, in diplomacy, in the Cabinet, in the Senate chamber, of the politics of America, from that day to this, is largely the history of that little band who assembled in Worcester. In the great emergencies of the country through which it has passed, when its diplomacy was to be conducted, in those dark days of the war, at the first court in Europe; when, after the war, its rights were to be maintained in that great tribunal at Geneva, a gentleman who had shown the American people his reliance on the sense of right and of justice against great majorities and great powers, was the gentleman whom his country selected for these important trusts. [Great applause.] When Massachusetts sent a man to the Senate chamber to conduct the great debate of liberty in the face of hostile parties, Charles Sumner, another of that little band, was chosen. [Great applause.] The forces—the political forces—which overthrew slavery and its two great armies,—the Whig and Democratic parties,—were organized by Henry Wilson, the young mechanic, who espoused the cause of liberty at the same time and place. [Loud applause.]

But, my friends, I have detained you longer with these reminiscences than I had any right to do, and I should much prefer to give place to some gentlemen who took part in these events, not as I did, as spectators merely, or voters, but as actors and leaders.

Mr. DOWNER. In one of those resolutions that I offered twenty-nine years ago, there is this expression: "That we express our gratitude to those faithful friends of freedom at Washington, Joshua R. Giddings, John G. Palfrey, and Amos Tuck." Mr. Tuck has never acknowledged this to me at all, but I have caught him here.

The PRESIDENT. We should all be extremely gratified to hear from Mr. Tuck, and I will say that it would be a personal favor to me, for it is a long time since I have had the pleasure of seeing him. I have not forgotten that his struggle was no trifle in New Hampshire. I remember that for a long time that State was considered by us as abandoned to the evil one, but, after all, New Hampshire came out bright, by the efforts of gentlemen like Mr. Tuck.

ADDRESS OF THE HON. AMOS TUCK.

I feel it to be a fearful thing to speak to these learned men of Massachusetts, but, born upon soil which was Massachusetts, as was the State of Maine before its admission to the Union, and now hailing from a State which is acknowledged to have done something toward building up Massachusetts, both in mind and material, I shall claim exemption from criticism,—all that exemption which would be accorded to one of your own sons who was feeble in speech and unlearned in the arts of oratory.

This convention is not one which assembles with the ordinary credentials, but we have credentials dating back thirty years. They are not made up by the officers of caucuses called within a week past; but those credentials consist of acts done many years ago, and no man can buy those credentials, any more than Simon Magus could buy the power to cast out devils. [Laughter and applause.] No one is rightfully a member of this convention or of this meeting, called by our friend Mr. Downer, to whom it may not be said by the Master, "Inasmuch as ye did it unto one of the least of these my brethren, ye did it unto me." If that can be said of those who were active thirty years ago, then they may come here.

Now, you are making up history here, and nobody can make up history better, or that is likely to last longer, than the people of Massachusetts; but will you please to take account of things that happened prior to 1848? Will you not bear in mind, Mr. Downer and gentlemen, that two years before, and more than two years previous to that date, people in the State of New Hampshire set an example of a conflict with party leaders that had never been set in this country before? [Applause.] We organized an opposition to the Democratic party in 1844-'5, which we have never given up to this day. [Renewed applause.] And in 1845, we made a declaration of principles that constituted the essence of the Republican party which was formed at Philadelphia eleven years later. I have in my pocket, gentlemen, a call which will prove the truth of what I say. Here is an original call for a convention on the 22d of February, 1845, signed by 263 Democrats, and drawn up by my friend John L. Hayes, now of Cambridge, and myself, in one of the jury-rooms in the Exeter court-house. It invites Democrats to assemble on the 22d of February, to take into consideration the condition of the party, and to make a declaration of sentiments in regard to the action which Mr. Hale had previously taken in opposition to the annexation of Texas. We were soon denounced by the great organs of the party, because we would not assent to the annexation of Texas, for the reasons given by Mr. Calhoun, or for any reasons whatever. We organized it as a movement of Democrats. Previous to that time, many men had remonstrated at different times against the action of the Democratic party in New Hampshire, which was the strongest Democratic State in the Union; but when they were denounced by the party leaders, and either passed over to the Abolitionists or to the Whig party, they acquiesced in being thus ranked. On the other hand, we insisted upon organizing as Democrats. We refused to leave the Democratic party, on account of our declaration of sentiments; we claimed that Anti-Slavery was true Democracy. We refused to leave the party, and we have refused to leave to this day, until we have got a majority of the Democracy of New Hampshire on the Republican side. [Applause.]

Well, gentlemen, I wish you to correct the history you are making. You have no right, permit me to say, to write on the page of history that the Republican enterprise in this country began in 1848. Previous to 1848, I have told you how we organized this opposition in New Hampshire in 1845. We began in '44. In '46, at the March election, the Independent Democrats held the balance of power between the Whig party and the Democratic party in New Hampshire. No election of Governor by the people having taken place, when the Legislature assembled in June of that year, we said to the Whigs, "We will put your man, Anthony Colby, into office as Governor of the State, if you will elect John P. Hale to the Senate." [Applause.] They said they would. This was in 1846. There was a vacancy in the House of Representatives, and they concluded, after Mr. Hale had been put in the Senate, to nominate myself for the House of

Representatives, and after several ineffectual efforts, I was elected to Congress in 1847,—one year before the Buffalo Convention. You had at that time elected John G. Palfrey as a regular Whig to the House of Representatives, and the Whigs of New Hampshire came in to the support of myself, simply because of my statement to Ichabod Bartlett, the President of the Convention, who was sent to consult with me, that I should expect, if elected, to be found voting with such men as Joshua R. Giddings and John G. Palfrey. [Applause.] I voted with them; but at the next election, the Whigs of Massachusetts would not re-elect Mr. Palfrey. Please to put that down on the record. [Laughter.] And in the revolution that took place in the United States, bear in mind that the humble State of New Hampshire placed the first anti-slavery Senator in the Senate of the United States. Joshua R. Giddings, elected as a Whig, John G. Palfrey, elected as a Whig, and your humble servant, elected as an Anti-Slavery, Independent Democrat, were the anti-slavery members of the House, who took their seats in the 30th Congress, which assembled in December, 1847. You formed your independent organization in Massachusetts in 1848. But when we organized in 1845, when we elected an anti-slavery man to the Senate in 1846, when we sent an anti-slavery man to the House in 1847, Charles Francis Adams, Charles Allen, Charles Sumner, and Henry Wilson stood well in the Whig party. But the Cotton Whigs rejected Dr. Palfrey, adopted General Taylor, and you rejected the Cotton Whigs. It was not until the next year that you pronounced the Whig party dissolved. We claim that we helped convert you. [Laughter and applause.] Please to put that down in the record of the history that you are making, because, while we cannot claim much in our little State, we are very jealous of what little we *can* claim. I say that here are the declarations carefully made at that Exeter

Reunion of Free-Soilers of 1848.   39

meeting, when we published an address and resolutions, and we had no occasion, up to the time of the formation of the Republican party, and in all our labors in the Republican party, and in all our votes in Congress or out, to cross a *t* or dot an *i* of what we wrote in February, 1845. And there is the document! Your patent was not taken out until 1848. [Laughter and applause.]

Now, let me give a little history of this document. It is the only one of the kind I could obtain, and let me tell you how I obtained it. So unpopular was our movement in 1844-'5, and so confident were the Democrats that the action of Mr. Hale and myself, and my friend Fogg,—long the editor of the "Independent Democrat" [applause], which was established in May, 1845, advocating Republican principles,—would be the end of us as men of any influence, that one Democrat in my town (Exeter) put away this call, and wrote upon the back of it (I will not detain you by reading it) enough to show that he kept it *in memoriam*, to condemn the men who signed this document, and who approved of the action that was taken by the convention. I appealed to his son (for the father has gone to his account) to allow me to see this. No, he could not let me see it. Well, I applied to him to purchase it, and I was obliged to pay a considerable sum of money before I could obtain it. [Laughter.] I value it very highly, and I shall take all the pains I can to see that it is preserved *in perpetuam*, in regard to the men of that time, and the events that then took place.

Now, Mr. Downer and Mr. Adams, pardon me for detaining the audience so long, and receive with all the favor you can my humble remarks. [Hearty applause.]

THE PRESIDENT. Among the gentlemen early connected with the Free-Soil movement, there was one with whom I had relations at one time very close in political affairs, and for whom I learned to have the most profound regard. I allude to STEPHEN C. PHILLIPS of Salem [loud applause],—a man who, in his public services, did not put himself forth in any way as a person to make a spectacle, but who, in the transaction of the business of the country, as in the details of life, maintained from the beginning to the end the highest possible character, not only as a merchant, but as a patriot. I had occasion, from time to time, to enter into consultations with him as to the course it was proper for us, then a small band, to take, under responsibilities of a very heavy character; and there never was a time in which his calm, moderate, but decided judgment did not have an influence, and an useful influence, upon our consultations. I believe we have here now present a son of Mr. Phillips, and I think, gentlemen, you will not find fault with me if I call upon him to say something in regard to the course that was taken, not only by his father, but followed up also by him in person.

ADDRESS OF THE HON. WILLARD P. PHILLIPS.

MR. PRESIDENT AND GENTLEMEN:—I know that I am called upon to-day to speak because I am the son of one who, in this movement, which was begun in '48, was present and active. I know that you call upon me to-day out of respect to him, and that the men who are here, who remember the campaign of '48, will never forget the services which he performed during that eventful period. [Applause.] It was my fortune, sir, in my younger days, before 1848, to be in my father's office, where one of my duties, apart from mercantile life, was to copy the various political correspondence, and to file the various political letters; and, sir, I recollect very well the various transactions in regard to the "Boston Whig," to which you have referred. I recollect a little paper which was printed in '45, and circulated under the title of "The Free State Rally and Texas Chain Breaker." I recollect, sir, your active movements, and the active movements of Judge Allen and my father, in regard to the annexation of Texas; what was done at the meeting in Faneuil Hall, which, sir, led directly, with those gentlemen, to their action in the Whig party in '46 and '47, when they became known as Conscience Whigs. From that time, when in our various conventions we used to rally to the defence of the Wilmot proviso, and resolve, "that we will support no man for office who is not known by his acts or recorded opinions to be opposed to the further extension of slavery," — from that time until Judge Allen and Henry Wilson appeared in the convention in '48, and announced that Massachusetts "spurned the bribe," and that the Whig party was dissolved, the action of those men who had acted with the Conscience Whigs was well known, and it was clearly understood, when the movement was made for the Buffalo Convention, that those gentlemen would be there. [Applause.] The history of that convention you have related so fully, that no one need say another word about it. But let me say this in regard to my father.

My friend here on my left (Mr. Tuck) has claimed early thunder. [Laughter.] Now, sir, you will recollect that in the campaign of '44, when New York voted on the Tuesday before Massachusetts, so that when we held the last rally previous to the election in Massachusetts, we were perfectly cognizant of what the result was, and that Henry Clay was defeated; but notwithstanding that, the Whigs were called upon to go up and deposit their votes for Mr. Clay. The meeting in Salem was held on Saturday evening, the last meeting before the election; and at the close of that meeting, at which my father presided, he came out on the platform and requested the gentlemen then present to vote on Monday for Henry Clay, but he wished to say that for himself it would be his last vote for a slaveholder for President, or for any other responsible office. [Applause.] That was the ground that he took then, and when 1848 came, he lived up to this pledge, and did not go back upon his words.

To a young man who is beginning, that campaign of '48 is a glorious reminder of what men of courage can do. It is a reminder of what they should do; and for my part, sir, I have learned this one lesson, which I have endeavored to follow through life, in politics especially, that there is one duty of all the young men and of all the old men, and that is to oppose improper and unfit nominations. [Applause.] On that lesson, sir, I have practiced, and I trust that in our future political action in this State, we may have the courage of the men of '48, and oppose at all times the nomination and election of improper candidates. [Applause.]

The PRESIDENT. We have here so many gentlemen on whom, perhaps, I have a right to call, that it is a little puzzling to determine whom to select first. But among the hard-working individuals who devoted themselves to the maintenance of the principles which they have carried into successful operation, I can specify one whose life, from his first coming into the service—and he was one of the earliest, I think, to abandon the Whig party—to the present, has been marked by steady and faithful devotion to the cause. I need only mention the name of Hon. FRANCIS W. BIRD. [Hearty and prolonged applause.]

ADDRESS OF THE HON. FRANCIS W. BIRD.

Mr. CHAIRMAN:—I have the right to claim the same exemption which the younger Mr. Hoar claimed, for, being very ill, I requested you not to call me out; and I am quite sure, if you had submitted the question to the audience, you would not have got the same response for me that you got in regard to him.

Reunion of Free-Soilers of 1848. 43

I am sorry I have not something better to say to-day. Indeed, I do not know that we are celebrating the Free-Soil organization of 1848. We are carried back two years before that. We are called upon to celebrate the organization of a party in New Hampshire two years previously. All I can say about that is, this is the first time I ever heard of it.* [Laughter.] I was at Buffalo in 1848, and occupied a room with you, Mr. President, if you remember, the night before the convention. We were crowded pretty close, and I was obliged to take a cot in your room. So enthusiastic was I then, that after I went home, I boasted that I had occupied a room with the next Vice-President of the United States. Unfortunately, it did not turn out so. I well remember the convention. I well remember the grand mass meeting over which you presided. I well remember that it happened, perhaps by the accident of my standing near you when you were called out to join the committee of conference, that you asked me to take your seat as presiding officer of that convention. I should probably have forgotten it but for this incident: As soon as I took your seat, those barn-burners flocked around me and said, "Don't let Fred. Douglass get the floor!" They didn't want a "nigger" to talk to them. [Laughter.] I told them we came there for free soil, free speech, and free men; and I gave a hint to Mr. Douglass, that if he would claim the floor when the gentleman who was then speaking gave it up, he should

---

* I did not mean that I was ignorant of, or had forgotten, the fact, that Mr. Hale was elected Senator, and Mr. Tuck, Representative, previous to 1848; but I did mean that I had never before heard it claimed that these sporadic occurrences entitled them to claim priority in the *organization of the Free-Soil party*. There was never any Free-Soil party, organized as such, in New Hampshire. Of course, I did not mean to deny to our New Hampshire friends the credit of having elected anti-slavery men, as such, just as we in Massachusetts elected John Quincy Adams and Horace Mann as *anti-slavery* Whigs; but I did mean that we in Massachusetts organized the first distinctive, efficient, permanent Free-Soil party. That is all. It may not be much; but that we did. F. W. B.

certainly have it. [Great applause.] He had the good sense—which our colored brethren do not always have—to make a two minutes' speech, and sat down amid great applause.

I find myself thinking a good deal, not only of what took place at Buffalo, but during the three subsequent years. You have spoken of the character of the convention at Buffalo, as composed of earnest, sincere, and self-forgetting men. If there ever was such a convention held in this country, that was one. So, also, I want to say, that if there ever was a political organization in this country composed of earnest, sincere, unselfish, self-forgetting men, it was the Free-Soil organization of 1848, '49, '50, and '51. [Applause.] I have seen a good deal of political organizations and political operations and political manipulations from that day to this, but I never knew such a set of men, associated for political effort, as the men who were associated in those four campaigns. I feel myself always wanting to name them. Samuel Hoar, Rockwood Hoar, Charles Allen, Stephen C. Phillips, Charles Sumner, Henry Wilson, John G. Palfrey, Edward L. Keyes, Erastus Hopkins, and a host of just such men, who entered into those campaigns with one single purpose, and that was, to carry out their convictions as to the policy of the country, without a thought of personal ambition,—I mean for those first four years,—without any aim, each for himself, inconsistent with the good of the cause. And that was the inspiration of that whole movement, up to the time of the election of Charles Sumner. We went into that campaign in 1850, as declared in our Free-Soil campaign paper,—I see one of my associates in the editorship of that paper here by my side, and I hoped he would be called upon to speak before I was—my excellent old friend (and I hope I may still be allowed to call him my friend), Hon. John B. Alley; he and I and Horace E. Smith, then of Chelsea, and now, I believe, of New York, were the editors of "The Free-Soiler," the campaign paper of that year,—we went into that campaign with the declared purpose of rebuking the author of the 7th of March speech, of repudiating in the name of Massachusetts the Fugitive Slave Law, and to elect a Free-Soil United States Senator. We declared that, so far as our alliance with the Democrats was concerned, we were ready to join with them in electing a Democratic State Government, just as our friend here said that they said in New Hampshire to the Whigs, "If you will give us John P. Hale for Senator, we will give you a Whig Governor"; just as Messrs. Morse and Townsend, the Free-Soilers in the Ohio Legislature, said to the Whigs, "If you will help us elect Joshua R. Giddings, we will give you the State offices"; and to the Democrats they said, "If you will help us to elect Salmon P. Chase, we will give you the State offices." Precisely that we said to our Democratic allies in Massachusetts: "We are here in the Legislature for one single purpose,—the election of an United States Senator. That Senator is to be Charles Sumner. Help us to elect him, and we will give you the State Government, and you must carry it on. You must take the entire Government,—the Governor and the entire State ticket,—and carry it on yourselves, and be responsible for it, and after the election we shall be in *statu quo ante bellum*, and have the liberty to criticize your administration just as freely as we did the Whig administration." That we laid down as our platform all through the campaign, and that we laid down as our claim after the Legislature met. Our Democratic friends declined to carry on the State Government without our aid, and in an evil hour we decided to take a part of the State offices, and having got a taste of blood, we never lost it. [Laughter.] It was that that degraded the coalition and debauched our Free-Soil party, and defeated us, as we deserved to be defeated, through the aid of our friends, Mr. Adams and Dr. Palfrey; and I have always been grateful to them for it, and have taken occasion frequently to acknowledge it. That coalition was perpetuated until we found ourselves in alliance with the Democratic party, after it had nominated Franklin Pierce for President on a pro-slavery platform; and then, when we attempted to keep up the relation as before, we were defeated, as we deserved to be. But never was there a party on the face of the earth, led, guided, controlled, and directed by braver and more self-sacrificing men, than the Free-Soilers from 1848 to 1851. [Loud applause.]

I am glad to be here, Mr. President. I wish I were able to say something more interesting and more instructive to this gathering. We shall never look upon each others' faces again. How many have gone in the past! How many of the brave, true, faithful men with whom we were associated, have gone to their reward! We are following them, one after another, to whatever reward awaits us. We shall never look upon each others' faces again. Three or four years ago, I proposed this gathering to General Wilson. He fell in with it very cordially, and we frequently spoke of it up to the time of his death; but it was never brought about until my friend, Mr. Downer, stopping me in his carriage one day on the street, proposed such a gathering here. It is good for us to be here. I wish we had two or three hours' more time to look into each others' faces, and to say a few more words of these pleasant reminiscences and of hope for the future. For one, my active days are over; but I have an earnest, profound faith in the principles of our old organization, and of the Republican party in its best days, when we were all proud to count it as the successor of the old Free-Soil party of Massachusetts. Honest men in the long run act together upon all grave public questions. [Applause.] We differ

somewhat, some of us, now; but I have an abiding faith,
Mr. President, that before I die, we, the old Free-Soilers
of Massachusetts, are yet to stand together, shoulder to
shoulder, in carrying out the principles of the Free-Soil
organization of 1848, '49 and '50, at the bottom of which
lay this great doctrine of the equal rights of all men before
the law. That I hold to be true Democracy. [Applause.]
To that Democracy I pledged myself in my youth; to
that,'as Whig, Free-Soiler, Republican, I gave the best
service of the vigor of my life; to that I will devote the
feeble strength of my old age, and I pray God to hasten
its triumph. [Great applause.]

The PRESIDENT. Hitherto we have had addresses
from gentlemen who have discoursed to you in a grave
manner, with weight and with effect. The time has now
come when I think it my duty to diversify it with a little
other matter. I believe Mr. Thomas Drew has a poem,
which he will read to you.

ADDRESS OF MR. THOMAS DREW.

I will detain the audience, at this late hour, but a very
few moments; but as Mr. Downer alluded to the spirit of
prophecy which was upon him in those early days, I
wish to read to you a few lines which form the conclusion
of a prophecy which I made in the "heart of the Commonwealth," a few days after the convention adjourned,
over which you had the honor to preside at Buffalo. It
so happened to me, that I was then a young man editing
a weekly newspaper at Worcester. Mr. Earle, the editor
of the old "Worcester Spy," asked me to take charge of
his paper during his absence at the convention, and I
reluctantly consented to do so. The first editorial written in Massachusetts, placing at the mast-head the names
of Van Buren and Adams, committing that paper

unreservedly and unequivocally to the support of those nominations, and renouncing all allegiance to the Whig party, was written by myself. It was very short, and may not be uninteresting on such an occasion as this.

"We place at the head of our columns to-day the nominations of the Buffalo Free-Soil Convention.

"They have been fairly made by the unanimous votes of the representatives of the advocates of Free-Soil, assembled from all the Free States, and, we doubt not, are the best that could have been made to secure the triumph of the principle of *no extension of slavery*.

"The letter of Mr. Van Buren will commend itself to all who may have had any doubt remaining as to his opinions upon this important subject. He has stated his views in a clear and candid manner, and they are such as will be responded to by every friend of freedom throughout the length and breadth of the land.

"The only issue now before the country, is *Freedom* or *Slavery*. The only parties are composed of the friends of slavery extension on the one hand, and the friends of freedom on the other. With the former we have always been at issue; towards the latter our sympathies have always tended, and in this important crisis in our history we feel a stronger disposition than ever to labor in the good cause. The nominations of the Buffalo Convention will receive our hearty support."

I wish also to read the concluding sentence of an editorial which I wrote for the "Christian Citizen," the weekly paper to which I referred, edited by "the learned blacksmith," who was at that time absent in Europe, which contains the prophecy to which I have alluded, and shows the inspiration under which the young men of Massachusetts worked at that time. They believed that the cause was of God, that it was to be triumphant, and that there was no sort of doubt in regard to its speedy success.

"The day of the bondman's redemption draws nigh. Through all the length and breadth of the land, the jubilant murmur is breaking, and *ere another generation shall have passed away*, the full glad chorus will arise that shall thrill the universe with joy, that the American people have decreed the *freedom* of the *slave*, and established the *freedom* of the *soil*."

Mr. President, the poem I am about to read is very short. I supposed that this would be an occasion when you would desire to indulge in some reminiscences of the past, and you must excuse whatever faults you may find in it, because it was written with the especial purpose of enlivening the seriousness to which you have referred as characterizing occasions like this.

> Now here at last, with hearts elate,
>   The Free-Soil veterans throng,
> Who led the fight in forty-eight
>   'Gainst tyranny and wrong.
>
> The curtain of the vanished Past,
>   To-day we draw aside;
> Our bread, once on the waters cast,
>   Returns with every tide.
>
> The memories of thirty years
>   Throng round this board to-day,
> With all the hopes, resolves, and fears
>   That marked the devious way
>
> By which God's Providence has wrought,
>   Through patriot blood and toil,
> The triumphs of the ends we sought,
>   In "Freedom and Free-Soil."
>
> In retrospect, we see the times
>   When ranks were thin and weak,
> And—closely drawn the party lines—
>   'T was heresy to speak.
>
> We hear the clarion tones once more
>   Of Sumner and of Mann,
> Of Allen, Webb, and Samuel Hoar,
>   Who led in Freedom's van.
>
> The stalwart form of Phillips, now,
>   From Salem town seems here,
> And Burlingame of dauntless brow,
>   With words of lofty cheer.

> The earnest words that Wilson spoke,
>   Our memories here recall;—
> Sturdy and tough as mountain oak,
>   Scorning all party thrall.
>
> John Andrew's earnest, honest brow
>   Gleams through the shadows dim,
> And the careworn, thoughtful face of Howe,
>   Ranges in line with him.
>
> One other name I here recall,
>   And then my task is done;
> The journalist, who toiled for all,—
>   We called him "Warrington."
>
> Of men less marked who fought the fight,—
>   How vain to speak their praise
> In the bright radiance of the light
>   Of these more hopeful days!

[Loud applause.]

Mr. DOWNER. Fellow Free-Soilers, the time has about arrived (hastened by the shower) to close this meeting. Before we separate, I wish to express the obligation I feel under to every one of you for this delightful revival of the memories of '48, and should our country hereafter be in deadly peril, may the crop of good seed then sown produce fruits for its salvation!

The PRESIDENT. I propose the health and long life of our generous host, Mr. Downer.

The company rose and responded to this sentiment with three hearty cheers, after which they repaired to the wharf and took the boat for the city, rejoicing in a day well and happily spent, and with a store of pleasant memories for future years.

SUPPLEMENTAL SPEECHES AND LETTERS.

The preceding pages contain a record of all that was said at the table. But there were very many present to whose voices the company would gladly have listened had there been time. Understanding that several gentlemen were prepared to speak, if called upon, Mr. Downer caused a circular to be sent to them, requesting them to write out their remarks for publication in the proposed report of the proceedings. In response to this invitation, the following addresses and letters have been kindly furnished:—

ADDRESS OF THE HON. JOHN B. ALLEY.

Twenty-nine years ago to-day, I had the high privilege of taking a seat in that famous Buffalo Convention, which ushered into being the renowned Free-Soil party. That conference convention, as it was called, in contradistinction to the mass convention, which assembled at the same time, sat with closed doors. It has been my fortune to sit in many conventions and deliberative assemblies, but never before or since in so interesting a body. It was composed mostly of representative men of three distinct political organizations, most of them able and distinguished, some of them illustrious, and all of them intensely earnest. The Democrats had met in national convention at Baltimore, and virtually repudiated the "Wilmot Proviso," and by its nominations, its action, its votes, and its platform, allied itself more thoroughly than ever to the slave power. The following month, the Whig party met in national convention at Philadelphia, and made, if possible, a still higher bid for slaveholding support, by refusing to put forth any platform, and nominating a Louisiana slaveholder, who had no political record whatever,—General Zachary Taylor, nominated solely for his military record and supposed devotion to the slave power. The dissenting Democrats, called "Barn Burners" in New York, entered their protest, and called a convention at Utica, and nominated Martin Van Buren for President. The anti-slavery Whigs, equally disgusted, were panting for an opportunity to record their emphatic protest, by uniting with all the other political organizations, and entering the contest with the battle-cry of freedom, and these memorable words, "Free Soil, Free Speech, and Free Men," inscribed upon their banner. These anti-slavery Democrats, anti-slavery Whigs, in combination with representative men of the old Liberty party, met together in that convention, determined to sink all minor differences to secure the one great object of a united opposition to the further increase of the slave power. It was difficult to agree upon a platform, with such discordant views upon political questions as characterized the antecedents of most of those in that convention. But they were wise, earnest, patriotic men, determined to agree. The platform was the work of Salmon P. Chase, who was the president of the convention. The resolutions, although written by Mr. Chase, were brought forward and presented by Benjamin F. Butler of New York, a distinguished lawyer, who had previously been in Mr. Van Buren's cabinet. He advocated them in a very able and eloquent speech, and after an exhaustive discussion, the most interesting it was ever my privilege to listen to, they were adopted. After their adoption came the tug of war, in the struggle for the nomination. All the "Barn-Burners" were for Mr. Van Buren, and to ask the Liberty party and "Conscience Whigs," as they were called, to vote for Martin Van Buren to promote anti-slavery principles, was requiring them to swallow a bitter pill. He, of all the statesmen of the country, was the most obnoxious to the anti-slavery sentiment. He alone, among the Presidents or candidates for the presidency, had dared to pledge beforehand his unalterable determination to resist, by every means in his power, every attempt to abolish slavery in the District of Columbia, and to interpose, if necessary, should Congress pass a law abolishing it, his executive veto. He also had given his casting vote in the Senate, authorizing breaking open the mails to purge them of anti-slavery publications. Added to all this, no one among the Democrats had been so obnoxious, politically, to the Whig portion of the convention, as Mr. Van Buren. The discussion upon the nominations was earnest, able, and at times very exciting. The friends of Mr. Van Buren claimed that he was all right then, whatever he had been before, and they plead most earnestly for his nomination, upon the ground that, with him as the nominee, we could control the electoral vote of New York, and that it would open the doors of all conventions and assemblages of "Barn Burners" to Free-Soil speakers, and nothing would indoctrinate the Democratic party with anti-slavery truth so much as the seizure of such an opportunity. With the determination of all to conquer their prejudices for the good of the cause, their reasoning prevailed, and Mr. Van Buren was nominated. Too much praise cannot be given to the Whig members of that convention, who so readily sacrificed their life-long prejudices in devotion to principle and patriotism. There was one man in that convention whom I especially desire to mention,— the Hon. Stephen C. Phillips. He, to my youthful mind, for I was a young man then, was the moral hero of that convention. A prominent, devoted, and popular Whig, with the certain prospect, as his friends all believed, of being the next Governor of Massachusetts, if he remained in the Whig party, he had been especially prominent in his denunciation of Mr. Van Buren as pre-eminently "the Northern man with Southern principles;" but when convinced of his duty, he hesitated not a moment, and I see him now, in my mind's eye, sitting by the side of Mr. Chase, as the vice-president of his State in the convention, watched by all at that anxious moment to learn how he would vote. When his name was called, I remember well his prompt response, in that loud, ringing voice of his, "Martin Van Buren." His response was a relief to the whole convention, and all felt that he, at least, was a patriot and statesman who knew his duty, and dared to do it. In that convention of personal sacrifice of feelings, prejudices, and prospects, no one surrendered more than Stephen C. Phillips.

In point of numbers, weight of character, and earnest purpose, no convocation of the people in this country, at that time, had ever been comparable to that assemblage at Buffalo. The record and results of that convention will live fresh in American history as long as the nation lasts.

LETTER FROM THOS. WENTWORTH HIGGINSON.

NEWPORT, R. I., August 23, 1877.

SAMUEL DOWNER, Esq.

DEAR SIR:—I was very much disappointed at being unable to attend your gathering of Free-Soilers, and thank you for asking me to write out the remarks I should have made. That is, unfortunately, a thing I never succeed in doing. It would be as easy for me to write out the remarks I should have made in Congress, had the Free-Soilers succeeded in electing me, in 1848, to represent the Essex District. I was then only a defeated candidate, and I was on this later occasion a reluctant absentee,—thus making no speech in either case. Had any been made, it would, doubtless, have included the assertion, that I was proud, in 1848, of being a Free-Soiler, and, in 1877, of having been one.

Very truly yours,

THOS. WENTWORTH HIGGINSON.

LETTER FROM EDWARD L. PIERCE, Esq.

MILTON, August 14, 1877.

DEAR MR. DOWNER:—You request me to put on paper the remarks which I should have made if there had been time to call me up at the "Reunion of the Free-Soilers of 1848," on the 9th instant. I cannot give them, for I had none prepared. Professional toils, which happened to press to the last moment, allowed me no opportunity to arrange in my mind the memories of that historic period; and I esteemed myself fortunate in remaining a listener during the interesting festival which we owe to your hospitality.

My own connection with the events you commemorated was but meagre. In 1848, I was a college youth, still in my teens. My first remarks in a political meeting were made that summer in a schoolhouse at Easton, the scene of early academic studies, where I was called up by Dr. Caleb Swan, at the close of his report as a delegate to the Buffalo Convention. That autumn I contributed several articles in favor of the new movement to the "Norfolk County Democrat," then conducted by Elbridge G. Robinson (an elder brother of William S.), and, returning to Brown University to begin my junior year, did what I could in our debating society, and in personal intercourse, to bring fellow-students to our side. My father, Colonel Jesse Pierce of Stoughton, who had been an anti-slavery Democrat, was, that year, a Free-Soil candidate for the Senate, associated on the ticket with Milton M. Fisher of Medway and Edward L. Keyes of Dedham. My elder brother, then twenty-three years old, since mayor of Boston and member of Congress, was very active in canvassing for the new party; and it was largely due to his efforts that the Free-Soilers carried, that year, the town of Stoughton, electing their representative.

On the evening of August 22, I attended, at Faneuil Hall, the ratification meeting, where Sumner presided, John A. Andrew read resolutions, and Richard H. Dana, Jr., David Dudley Field and Joshua Leavitt spoke. Sumner, whom I did not then personally know, was in the prime of manly beauty and power; and I well recall him, wearing his blue coat and gilt buttons (a favorite dress of that period), and waving his cane as he cheered, and turning now and then his eye to an enthusiastic citizen in the left gallery, who was clapping his hands with great energy. My brother and myself attended, as volunteers, the first Free-Soil county convention at Dedham, called to elect delegates to the Buffalo Convention, and were admitted as delegates, in the absence of any regular representative from our town. The occasion is now somewhat indistinct in memory, but I remember the trenchant speech of Keyes, and the attractive presence of William

Richardson of Dorchester, as he moved up and down the aisles. Such is the brief record of what a Free-Soil minor saw in 1848. Two years later, in 1850, the first year of my majority, in company with a fellow-student of the Harvard Law School, my much-valued friend, John Winslow, now a distinguished lawyer of New York, I addressed several Free-Soil meetings, the first being at Newton Upper Falls, and from that time continued to do what I could for the cause, through newspaper articles and campaign addresses.

At the "Reunion," held under your auspices, the chiefs who led in the great movement were duly commemorated,—Palfrey, S. C. Phillips, Adams, Sumner, Wilson, Mann, E. Rockwood Hoar, Giddings, and Chase. Mr. Wilson, in his history, has given these an enduring fame. But behind these ever-honored names were a great number of true men, without whose devotion, capacity for organization, determined purpose and inspiring speech, these leaders would have failed. I delight to recall some of this class, who lived in the southern part of the Commonwealth, with which I am most familiar. Among them were F. W. Bird of Walpole, who, in the Legislature, at that early period, was a fearless "Conscience Whig"; Edward L. Keyes and John Shorey of Dedham, Milton M. Fisher of Medway, Otis Cary of Foxborough, Dr. Appleton Howe of Weymouth, Cornelius Cowing of West Roxbury; and in Dorchester, William Richardson (an able lawyer, with remarkable gifts in conversation), Asaph Churchill, Samuel Downer, Jr., Ebenezer Clapp, Henry O. Hildreth, and Rev. Nathaniel Hall, a clergyman who never counted the cost when a moral question was at stake. In Plymouth County were John A. Andrew of Hingham, Seth Webb, Jr., of Scituate, Jesse Perkins of North Bridgewater, and Morton Eddy of Bridgewater, the last being one of the first two in his town who voted for freedom in 1840, and one of eleven in 1843. In Bristol County were ex-Governor Marcus Morton, his son Nathaniel, who had a genius for the law such as few lawyers have, and who was also a very effective political speaker (two other sons of the ex-Governor were distinguished by like zeal in the cause,—Marcus, Jr., in Boston, and James H. in Springfield); also Edmund Anthony and S. O. Dunbar of Taunton—the last still living; Laban M. Wheaton of Norton; and John A. Kasson, then a young lawyer of New Bedford, who has since won a national reputation. But there is one whom I cannot dismiss with the bare mention of his name,—Dr. Caleb Swan of Easton, to whose inspiration I owe much for my early interest in the good cause. He died in 1870, at the age of seventy-six, after fifty-four years of exacting professional toils, continued to the end. He swept, in his practice, a territory of remarkable extent, comprising his own town, the four Bridgewaters, Raynham, Taunton, Norton, Stoughton, and Sharon.

He began his anti-slavery work in 1841, in association with his relative, George W. Johnson, once a Liberty-party candidate for Governor of this State, and now a resident of Buffalo. In his professional rides, in dwellings, on highways, in halls, school-houses, and church vestries, Dr. Swan made converts to the faith. His voice was earnest and deep-toned, and he had magnetic power on the platform and in conversation. He had skill in organization, securing the election of a Liberty-party representative in 1842 (who came near being speaker) and a Free-Soil representative in 1850. He often led a forlorn hope as a candidate, but refused nominations likely to be followed by an election, except in a single instance, near the close of his life. I remember that several times Mr. Sumner spoke with enthusiasm of his zeal and good sense and hearty ways.

Other parts of the Commonwealth were not less fertile in true men than the southern. There was John M. Earle in Worcester; William S. Robinson in Lowell; William Claflin in Hopkinton; John B. Alley in Lynn; Daniel W. Gooch in Melrose; James M. Stone in Charlestown; Thomas Russell, then a student, in Plymouth; Gershom B. Weston in Duxbury; James T. Robinson in Adams; Daniel W. Alvord in Greenfield; Erastus Hopkins, Oliver Warner, and Abijah W. Thayer in Northampton; Estes Howe in Cambridge; the Bowditches, Samuel E. Sewall, William B. Spooner, Samuel G. Howe, Elizur Wright, Dr. James W. Stone, Anson Burlingame, Theodore Parker, and many more of their type, in Boston and its neighborhood. Nor can we forget the poets, whose harps were ever responsive to our cause,—Whittier, Longfellow, and Lowell; or the noble women, like Mrs. Child and Mrs. Stowe, who, in tale, or verse, or earnest appeal, inspired their generation. But I must not prolong the enumeration. Time would fail me to tell of Gideon, and of Barak, and of Sampson, and of Jephthah, who, through faith, stood firm for the freedom of a race; out of weakness were made strong; waxed valiant in fight; breasted social and political proscription; served faithfully to the end a cause as grand as any for which martyrs ever died. But all such, whether commemorated or not, whether permitted with mortal eyes to witness the grand consummation of all their toils and self-sacrifice, or dying without a glimpse of the promised land, deserve, and will receive, the gratitude of mankind.

Yours truly,

EDWARD L. PIERCE.

ADDRESS OF THE HON. MILTON M. FISHER OF MEDWAY.

Mr. PRESIDENT:—Our minds, on this occasion, instinctively revert to the political scenes and events of 1848, and especially to the Buffalo Convention, and matters incident thereto.

It will be recollected that, previous and up to 1848, there had been an earnest and vigorous discussion, in Congress and out, upon what was called the "Wilmot Proviso," which was simply a resolution offered in the House of Representatives by Mr. Wilmot, a Democrat from Pennsylvania, to prohibit the further introduction of slavery into new territory.

It was foreseen that this question would enter very largely into the canvass for President in that year. Both Democrats and Whigs had held their national conventions, and nominated, the former, General Cass, and the latter, General Taylor. The former was a Northern "doughface," or trimmer, and the latter a Southern slaveholder, and the hero of the Mexican war, which had been waged to add new territory to be carved into new slave states. Both Cass and Taylor were committed against this proviso of freedom.

But, in both the Whig and the Democratic parties, there were many in the Free States who had the courage to say to the slave power, "Hitherto shalt thou come, but no further; and here shall thy proud waves be stayed." Several delegates in these conventions had bolted the nominations, and conspicuously, in this State, Charles Allen and Henry Wilson. After conference with each other, the "friends of Free Soil for Free Men" called a convention, to be held at Buffalo on the 9th of August, 1848, to adopt the platform of a new party, and to nominate candidates for President and Vice-President. It was my good fortune, Mr. President, to be associated with yourself and Mr. Wm. J. Reynolds, now deceased, as the three delegates from Norfolk County (as it was), representing, as we did, the three constituent elements that were to be fused into the new party; to wit, the "Conscience Whigs," the "Barn Burners," and the "Liberty Party." This old Liberty party,—formed in 1840, composed of men of the most uncompromising character, who had been hammered and welded together by the bitterest opposition to the anti-slavery cause,—often deceived by the anti-slavery professions of mere politicians, at first distrusted the sincerity of men, who, with new-born zeal, began to shout "Free Soil," and doubted whether the Buffalo Convention would be any better than a "big fizzle," as its enemies predicted.

But the eventful day came, and the "men of faith" were there; among them Chase and Giddings of Ohio, Wm. Jackson and Leavitt of Massachusetts, Fessenden and Appleton of Maine, Stewart and Green of New York, and many others. The new enthusiasm of bolting anti-slavery Whigs and Democrats soon fused with the old fire of "Liberty men," and the union of sentiment and purpose was complete, and found fit expression in a common platform of principles and measures, unanimously adopted, and applauded to the echo by thousands of sturdy yeomen from all the Free States.

But in the matter of candidates, a division was early foreseen. John P. Hale, who had already done valiant service in Congress, was the favorite of the Liberty men, Judge McLean of the Whigs, and Van Buren of the Democrats. It was soon learned, through Mr. Chase, that Judge McLean would not accept the nomination, and this narrowed the contest to the other two, and when the vote was declared, Van Buren had a majority of twenty-two votes. The excitement was intense. The "Barn Burners," who saw in it the death of Cass, were jubilant. The "Conscience Whigs," disappointed at the withdrawal of Judge McLean, now reluctantly accepted the situation, while the "Liberty men" were stunned with grief and momentary confusion. No public man had been more obnoxious to the Whigs or the Abolitionists than Van Buren. It was hard to believe he had made much progress in his views or position upon public affairs, since he said, in advance of his election to the Presidency, he would veto any bill for the abolition of slavery in the District of Columbia. But Mr. Van Buren had written confidential letters, and David Dudley Field, B. F. Butler of New York, and John Van Buren pledged him to accept the nomination squarely upon the platform, and that was urged as all that could be asked.

Among the "Liberty men," who had often been betrayed, as they thought, by public men, there was anxiety and distrust. Their confidence was not easily won. The question went round in the convention of delegates, "Must we give up our party name and organization, and, more than all, support the 'Little Magician'?"

And now, Mr. President, an incident occurred which no Liberty-party delegate in that convention can ever forget. In this dilemma, the stalwart form of Joshua Leavitt, the editor of the "Emancipator," a leader of the advanced minds in the cause of freedom, rose up, and Mr. Chase, who presided in this convention, announced that Mr. Leavitt had the floor.

All eyes were turned to him as the great expounder of the Liberty-party policy. He began his speech perfectly calm and self-possessed. He referred to the struggles and sacrifices of those whom he represented, the tenacity with which they held their principles, and their devotion to the cause of human freedom, and their almost idolatrous attachment to John P. Hale, who had already been nominated by them for the

Presidency. He referred to their deep regret and disappointment at the result of the ballot just declared, but suddenly he exclaimed in a voice of thunder and lofty exultation, "The Liberty party is not dead, but TRANSLATED."*

Such shouts and cheers as came from all parts and parties in the house, when the old Liberty Guard magnanimously gave up their name, their party, and their candidate for the cause, were not surpassed by any of the many eventful and thrilling incidents at this great gathering. While your own honored name, Mr. Chairman, as candidate for Vice-President, did much to harmonize the various elements in the convention and among the people, that of Van Buren, it must be confessed, was a wet blanket to the ardor and zeal of many of the Whigs who started well in the Free-Soil movement. With Judge McLean as a candidate, Stephen C. Phillips had certainly been chosen the next Governor of Massachusetts.

I must beg your indulgence, Mr. President, as I relate one other incident, of which I was an eye-witness. On the morning of the convention, as I entered from a side street one of the principal avenues of the city, leading up from the Western steamboat landing, I saw a great crowd of stalwart men, brown with toil, and apparently belonging to the most intelligent class of farmers, who had just landed from one of the steamers from Cleveland, Ohio. At the same time, coming in an opposite direction, from the railroad station, I observed a tall, broad-shouldered man, with a brown duster and carpet-bag, walking in the middle of the street, whom I at once recognized as the indomitable Joshua R. Giddings, who had just arrived from Washington to attend the great meeting. At the same time, he was seen by this crowd of Buckeyes, most of whom were his constituents in old Ashtabula County and the Western Reserve. They rushed upon him almost *en masse*, without ceremony or introduction, shaking him by the hand, or getting hold of him as best they could, until the street was so blocked up that Mr. Giddings motioned to them to pass into a side court. Here he gave these sturdy pioneers of freedom a full opportunity to exchange salutations and congratulations with him upon the auspicious events now transpiring. As Mr. Giddings inquired after friends and families in Ohio, and as to the progress of the good cause at home, I was transfixed with amazement, and delighted as well, to see such an enthusiastic greeting with such a multitude of people, who, in their intense familiarity, seemed to belong to one great family, of which Mr. Giddings was the beloved patriarch.

---

* This sublime and felicitous declaration of Rev. Dr. Leavitt at Buffalo was subsequently quoted by Charles Allen, at the State Free-Soil Convention at Boston, and was most enthusiastically applauded. Henry Wilson in his "Rise and Fall of the Slave Power," Vol. II., page 159, appears to attribute this sentiment as original with Judge Allen, but this is a mistake.

After the nominations had been made, our "Barn-Burner" friends, who addressed the mass convention, were particularly happy. David Dudley Field, then a young lawyer in New York, of great promise, made at the mass convention a noble speech for the cause and for Mr. Van Buren. He began with the quotation from Shakespeare in "Richard the Third," and applied it with great pertinence and force to the successful nomination of the favorite candidate of the "Barn Burners,"—

> "Now is the winter of our discontent
> Made glorious summer by this son of York,
> And all the clouds that lower'd upon our house
> In the deep bosom of the ocean buried!"

Other incidents of this eventful occasion might be mentioned, but I forbear. The history of the party then formed is but partly written as yet. The great measure adopted was to restrict slavery to its existing limits, and this has not only been accomplished, but every inch of national soil is free soil, and trodden only by free men.

ADDRESS OF JOHN N. BARBOUR OF CAMBRIDGE, MASS.

Mr. DOWNER:—When I received your kind invitation to attend this gathering of veterans at your beautiful garden, I was told the object was to relate some reminiscences of the past, connected with the emancipation of our slaves,—one of the most glorious events of history. I turned over some of the leaves of memory, and found myself in my counting-room in Boston, forty-eight years ago, conversing with a young stranger, who was seeking a place in which to deliver an address on the subject of slavery. The earnestness of his manner, and the striking beauty of his countenance, interested me. I inquired his name. He told me it was Garrison. I asked him if he had been imprisoned in Baltimore for attacking that institution. He said he was the man. Being myself a young man of generous impulses, as I believed, I grasped his hand with warm sympathy, gave him a hearty welcome, and promised to aid him in his work of philanthropy. I applied to a deacon of a Baptist church, of benevolent tendencies, who assured me there would be no difficulty in procuring the house for that cherished purpose. A short time elapsed, when I inquired of him at what time the lecture was to be delivered; he told me the house could not be had, because the young man was crazy! Supposing that persecution and imprisonment might have had so sad an effect upon an ardent mind, I rested there. After every meeting-house had been refused, I learned that an address on that subject was to be made in the building at the corner of Congress and Milk streets, popularly styled "Infidel Hall," where the celebrated Abner Kneeland then proclaimed his peculiar views.

Being desirous of hearing what that "crazy man" had to say, I attended the meeting. I listened to the impassioned eloquence of the youthful orator, as he portrayed the wrongs and sufferings of the slave. Bound by no party affiliations, acknowledging no master but my Creator, I then and there decided that no act or word of mine should ever sanction or sustain such an atrocious system,—that eternal hostility should mark my course towards the disreputable institution of human bondage.

What could be done? I found the avenues to social, moral, pecuniary, political, religious influence were all permeated by its wonderful power, and woe to the young man who would try to stem the torrent! Some of us concluded to accept the situation, and sow the seed for a future crop. We found great need of a class of workers in humble and unpleasing positions. We established meetings for discussion in our various localities, hired halls, and printed notices, and having provoked the community with our unpopular principles, put our hands in our pockets and paid the deficiencies. We established newspapers which we well knew would not pay, published them till our funds were exhausted, and let them die only to renew the conflict and the expenditure year after year.

The noble James G. Birney of Kentucky was nominated for the Presidency by the Liberty party, after years of fearful struggle, and we saw in the dim distance the break of day. The Free-Soil movement, with its dubious elements of compromise for the overthrow of the "giant crime," under the lead of one in whom we had but little confidence, was presented by our leaders. Could we sanction it for its expected results? We supported it with misgiving, and in its action we found a power that might be utilized. "The nature of things" inaugurated the Republican party, which we accepted under protest, with the certainty that restriction of slavery ensured its death. Were we mistaken? In one respect we were. Some of the leaders of that party repudiated the idea that the inexorable logic of events made so plain to the slave owner, and even proposed to perpetuate slavery by ingrafting it into the Constitution, rather than have trouble about it.

The "God of Providence," who writes history even now, determined differently. The slave power in its madness struck the blow, and became a suicide. The cherished idol of the South was plucked from the vitals of the nation, and left its bleeding heart exposed to a wondering world. The institutions of two hundred years were changed by a proclamation! Our wounds are not yet healed; we will do all that is consistent with the great underlying principles of human freedom to heal them; but these principles must be sustained, if we will fulfil the mission that the Great Disposer has appointed for us.

ADDRESS OF JOHN WINSLOW, Esq., OF BROOKLYN, N. Y.

MR. CHAIRMAN AND GENTLEMEN FREE-SOILERS OF 1848 :—This is naturally an occasion of exultation and reminiscence. What the Free-Soilers of 1848 contended for has been accomplished, and more. In the dark days, when the slave power overshadowed the land, and was felt as a political force in all departments of the Government, he who became a Free-Soiler was sure to take his place and lot with the minority.

That minority was not inspired by any prospect of early success. Its inspiration was its principles. It was earnestly believed by the men of '48, whose deeds we commemorate, that the life-saving principles of the Republic, as laid down in the Constitution and in the Declaration of Independence, were sacrificed to the demands of slavery. The slave power was reaching out in all directions, through commercial channels and by political and social agencies, to assert its supremacy as a dominant element in the country. It was not content to insist upon its status in the several States, but was looking over into the Territories, whose regions have since become States, with covetous eyes.

It took the ground, with Calhoun as a leader, that the Constitution protected slavery and the right to establish it in the Territories as well as in the States of the Union.

All the powers of the Federal Government were invoked to maintain this position.

In pursuance of this aggressive policy, we saw such enactments as the Fugitive Slave Law, the decision of the Supreme Court in the Dred Scott case, when Chief Justice Taney, in an *obiter dictum*, declared that the slave and colored man had no rights which the whites were bound to respect. We saw, alas! Daniel Webster, on the 7th of March, 1850, in his place in the Senate, bending to the pro-slavery storm, and making concessions which humiliated him and the country. That 7th of March speech makes us wish the great man had completed his political record before the weakness of that day.

The Free-Soilers of 1848 took extremely conservative ground. Their movement was not against slavery as it was in the States, but, in the main, against its aggressive policy for its expansion in the Territories. The "Wilmot Proviso," and all similar propositions, sought chiefly to save the West and the Northwest, not then formed into States.

I have said this is naturally an occasion for exultation. It is so because we have seen the principles of 1848 triumph, not only in the

Territories, but, by the exercise of the war power, in all the States of the Union. What the war power did has been ratified by amendments of the Federal Constitution, and of the Constitutions of the old Slave States. As a result, we have the spectacle of a great nation, with a population of more than 44,000,000 of people, all free, in place of a nation which, in 1848, had within its limits 4,000,000 of slaves The aggressive, dominant slave power has disappeared as a force in our politics.

With these results assured, it does not require the prophetic voice to trace in the bright outlines of the future a new and grander career, in the pursuits of industry and peace, for our common country.

This is also a day of most interesting reminiscence. It is fitting that here and now we remember the heroic men of 1848. Some of these now among the dead have already been mentioned. As a townsman and neighbor, I well remember Horace Mann and William Jackson, both then of Newton. Before the agitation of 1848, Horace Mann had profoundly impressed the public mind as an educator and director in educational affairs in Massachusetts.

On his return from Europe, he wrote the memorable Seventh Annual Report as Secretary of the State Board of Education, giving his views of some of the superior methods of education as he had observed them in Prussia. In that report, he compared the Prussian system with that in Boston, which drew out the reply of the thirty-one schoolmasters of Boston, who seemed to think their vindication in order. Mr. Mann's famous answer, and the controversy that followed, disclosed to the country that in him we had a controversialist of unsurpassed ability. When Mr. Mann joined the movement of 1848, he did so with all his might. I have never known a more effective or clearer-sighted moral force in our politics than Horace Mann.

William Jackson of Newton was early in the field as an anti-slavery man. In the days of the Liberty party, which supported James G. Birney for President in 1844, William Jackson was active and prominent as a leader in that organization. He was an able merchant, and ever ready to give his means to the cause he loved. When the Free-Soil movement was organized, Mr. Jackson naturally took his place in it as a worker and leader. He regarded it as an outgrowth of the Liberty party, whose principles he loved so well. He hailed with delight the new and able accessions to the anti-slavery ranks which the Free-Soilers brought into the field. There was no man in the days of '48 whose judgment was more respected or whose advice was more sought for than William Jackson's. I may be permitted to refer to my own father, now deceased, as a townsman, friend, and co-worker with Mr. Jackson.

I leave for others the mention of such men and leaders as Sumner,

Wilson, Allen, Leavitt, Hopkins, and many others now gathered to the fathers. These, and such as these, are among our honored dead.

While, in a technical sense, the name of John Quincy Adams, who died in February, 1848, does not find a place in the list of Free-Soilers, yet it is true that his counsels and teachings, through a long and eventful political life, were inspiring sources of the Free-Soil doctrine.

While we thus reverently name the dead, it is right to refer to the living who were active and influential among the men of '48.

We are reminded by their presence here of the distinguished services of Judge Hoar; of his brother, your Senator; of Mr. Downer, our generous host; of the veteran Bird, who has fought a good fight, and who is, I know, proud of this occasion, and of the history that makes it; of Henry L. Pierce, an eminent merchant, lately mayor of Boston, and more recently a representative in Congress; and of his brother, E. L. Pierce, always fervent and steadfast in the faith, and among the ablest of its advocates. He may justly count it not among the least of the honors that have come to him in professional and political life, that he enjoyed the warm friendship and perfect confidence of Charles Sumner to the end, and is named by him in his will as one to take charge of his literary work, and put it in abiding form.

We may also refer to the honorable gentleman who is our presiding officer, as one who did valiant work in the days of '48. Though honors of wider significance have since come to him, I venture the opinion that in no part of his political record does he find profounder satisfaction than in that made as a Free-Soiler of 1848.

I see before me Governor Claflin, who was foremost among the faithful, and who has since been honored by Massachusetts as Governor, and now as member-elect of Congress. As I look through this hall, other names occur, such as Sewall, the learned and judicious legal adviser *in re* fugitive slave cases, and kindred matters. I note also the presence of Alley, Davis, Thompson, Clarke, Thayer, Grover, Wood, Gooch, Gould, Taft, Allen, and many others who are entitled to honorable mention.

Among the absent, let us not forget Whittier, who all his life has nobly sung the songs of freedom and of peace; nor the names of Bacon, Pettee, and Rice, co-workers with Jackson of Newton. H. B. Stanton, now of New York, will be remembered. As standing afar off, leading the van, and encouraging, in a prudent and careful way, what they thought was good and promising in the Free-Soilers, and urging them on to advanced positions, we must not forget the names of Phillips and Garrison.

In the course of nature, the men of '48 now living must soon take their places by the side of those of their coadjutors who have gone before. Cicero, in his essay, "*De Senectute*," takes the view, that among the felicities of the future life is the knowledge that one will have that his memory is cherished affectionately and with respect in the world he once lived in. Have we not reason to hope that, if such be one of the rewards of well-doing, the Free-Soilers of 1848 will enjoy that felicity?

Thanking you, gentlemen, for your kind attention, and you, Mr. Downer, for making this reunion and historic occasion possible, I give way to others who, I am certain, will entertain us with more of reminiscence and discussion.

ADDRESS OF THE HON. JAMES N. BUFFUM.

Mr. PRESIDENT:—I am happy to be present on this occasion to meet so many of the old friends of human freedom, and to congratulate ourselves upon the great work which has been achieved through the united efforts of all who have labored to make our country free. We come here, not for self-gratification, or for political advancement, but to look each other in the face, to shake hands once more in cordial, loving sympathy, and to arouse the old patriotic fires; to keep alive that love of God and man that burned so bright in the early days of our consecration; and, above all, to thank God that he has permitted us to labor in the great and glorious cause of freedom.

When we look back to the days when William L. Garrison began his work against slavery,—a work, all things considered, of greater magnitude than anything that has ever been accomplished in *this*, if not in any other country,—we are appalled in its contemplation; the brain grows dizzy over it, and we know that no human power could ever have accomplished it; we know that nothing short of the most self-sacrificing and devoted labor of wise and patriotic men and women, aided by the powers above, could have made that work triumphant. At that time, slavery was so interwoven into all our institutions, religiously, politically, and pecuniarily, that it defied all power, human and divine. Henry Clay said "that two hundred years had sanctioned and sanctified human slavery, and no power on earth could overthrow it." It was recognized in the Constitution of the United States; cherished and protected by State laws more cruel and diabolical than ever before disgraced our statute-books. These laws made it a crime to teach a slave to read the name of the God who made him,—one thousand dollars fine for the first offence, and death for the second. Men were loaded with chains and fetters, branded with hot irons,—the names of the owners burned deep into their quivering flesh,—and if any dared to run away from their cruel task-masters, they were hunted down with bloodhounds and returned. Time would fail me to describe the atrocities and horrors of the slave system. All this system of despotism was sanctioned by both Church and State, when a few patriotic men and women, inspired with justice and love, went forth in the strength which a noble cause always inspires to work its overthrow. Never since the days of Thermopylæ, when that little Spartan band threw themselves into that deadly breach, has the world witnessed a more sublime consecration. It was the sacrificing of all that men hold dear on the altar of humanity, the giving up of all political prospects, all religious recognition, all social enjoyment, and to be counted a fool, that our country might *indeed* be made *free.*

How well and how truly they have accomplished their work, let this large and happy assembly answer. Let the four millions, whose chains have been broken, speak. Let the glad notes of these enfranchised millions proclaim the magnitude and the glory of this hour, which we are permitted to see,—when our flag waves over a free and enlightened people, and the sun does not rise on a slave, nor set on a slave-master. But, friends, let us not be satisfied to retire from the field where we have done such good service, but let us remember that "the price of liberty is eternal vigilance"; that it is only as we are watchful and vigilant that we can prevent the encroachments of despotism. We have gained much, but there remains much more to be accomplished. There are still wrongs to be righted, evils to be encountered, which will tax the stoutest hearts, and require the strongest nerves to assail. Let us not forget that the grand idea which lies at the basis of our institutions, as well as that of the Christian religion, is the "equality of the human race"; *equal rights* and *equal burdens* should be the motto of every friend of his race.

At a time like this, when God has prospered us as he has no other nation; when he has opened the windows of heaven and poured us out blessings so thick and so fast that we have not room to receive them; when the West is full of provisions, sufficient for two or three countries like ours; when the East is full of all kinds of goods to wear; the North and the South are running over with material blessings, our banks flooded with money, cheaper than ever before known in this country,—we should not look each other in the face despondingly. No! let us once more put on the harness for a new fight against all forms of oppression. I am, perhaps, the oldest in this great conflict with slavery now present, with the exception of one, having labored since 1831, and yet I do not feel weary in well-doing, and I shall consider myself happy if I can continue to work on to the end. I see in this assembly Samuel E. Sewall, Esq., whom I recognize as one of the earliest of the anti-slavery friends, whose labors and wise counsel made it possible for the organization of the political parties which followed moral agitation. I do not stand here to criticise the labors of any, or to say who has done the most to bring about these grand results, but to say that no one has worked earnestly in vain,— all was needed. He who quarries the granite, and shapes it to fit its proper place in the great temple of freedom, is no less a useful workman than he who was the architect and first conceived of its beautiful proportions, and shaped them into form for the admiration of men. I hope the time will come when all artificial distinctions will be done away; when a better culture, broader opportunities for labor, and better knowledge of true relation of capital and labor, will reconcile all disturbing elements in our land; when every class, grade, and condition shall enjoy equal blessings, as well as carry equal burdens.

Mr. President, I thank Mr. Downer, through you, for his kind invitation to be with you, and although I was not so much of an active politician as some present, I trust I did my share to make a public sentiment against slavery, without which no political party could have existed.

ADDRESS OF CHARLES W. SLACK.

Mr. CHAIRMAN AND GENTLEMEN:—My interest in the Free-Soil movement of 1848 grew out of my Democratic education, that this was a government of the *people*; that the *people* should rule; and that the mass of the *people* had their interests consulted in governmental affairs. I was prone to ask my respected father whether the four millions of "people" at the South, held in bondage, had no claims upon our consideration. The formation of the Free-Soil party was the occasion for a practical interest in those "people," impelled by the logic of consistency and the sentiment of humanity. It was a great satisfaction to belong to a party that had a high moral idea. I well remember how enthusiastic I was that the blot of human servitude should be removed from our otherwise creditable national escutcheon. I was joyed to find so many other young men sharing with me that feeling. Those men, now grown to maturity's estate, will be ever most dear to me, whether in the living presence, or only as a memory and an inspiration. We resolved we would give no rest to our feet, no silence to our tongues, till the great task was accomplished. To this aim we sacrificed business, ambition, convenience, and social position. To this end we were ready for any or all political combinations that would the speedier and more surely bring the consummation desired. We fought long,—I know it was well,—and, in the result, we have a right to be prouder than over any other achievement of life.

The period of our national history from 1845 to 1865 can never be complemented for sublime and ennobling disinterestedness. The sacrifice of old political relations; the ardor for new contests which followed recurring defeats; the grand enthusiasm of the first Republican campaign under Fremont; the anxious devotion to principle under the leadership of Lincoln; the noble rising of the country for its imperilled nationality; the vigor of the maintenance of the armies; the hot earnestness for the enrolling of the negroes; the transcendent glory of the emancipation of the slaves; the sublime vindication of our Republic in the final result of the war,—all these were part of the honors that came to the little band that stood upon principle in 1848. Such aims, enthusiasms, and results can hardly, in the nature of things, occur a second time, in so limited a period, in our history. I would not part with my share in the joy of this great endeavor for all the wealth that a close business application for the same period could bring.

And this last suggestion prompts me to ask whether an indifference to great moral issues in national life ever is recompensed. I knew many a young man of my own age who had no interest in the problem we sought to work out; they toiled and wrought, and comparative prosperity came to them, while the claims of a higher public life, and the reconciliation of our national practice with our profession, were matters of little concern. I have seen many of these men brought to adversity, even to poverty, through the vicissitudes of business. Permanent success has not been theirs, and when this was denied, no hallowing came to them through the remembrance of a devoted interest in the liberty of bondmen, or the redemption of a blighted land. Nor have all the soldiers in Freedom's cause been blessed with this world's goods; but they have that priceless reward which cannot be taken from them,—the knowledge that, by their devotion, consistency, and endurance, they have seen the glory of God in the removal of slavery from our land, and may yet realize the promise of a homogeneous, happy, prosperous people. Heaven grant that this may be our final satisfaction ere we pass from the cares of earth!

LETTER FROM DR. EDWARD JARVIS.

DORCHESTER, August 16, 1877.

MY DEAR MR. DOWNER:—I regretted my inability to attend your celebration of the twenty-ninth anniversary of the Free-Soil movement. I was at Provincetown, the extreme end of Cape Cod, on that day; but there I thought of you and of your doings with great interest and sympathy.

Afterward, at the house of Judge Scudder, in Barnstable, I saw the full account of the proceedings of the day at the Landing.

The feelings of that time—1848—are still fresh in my mind and heart. I had for years watched the progress of Southern aggression, and in sorrow wondered at our Northern apathy and willingness to submit to it.

As the South always said, "This is our last request or demand," we acquiesced for the sake of peace. But when they had secured their gain, and we were going on unsuspectingly, they put forth another *last demand*, with the same assurance, that never again would they disturb the peaceful compact.

So they went on with renewed exactions from year to year, from generation to generation, and we with renewed and renewing submission. There seemed to be no end of the Southern power of self-expansion, and of our self-contraction of spirit,—all for the sake of peace.

The South had had all, in its own way, from 1789 to 1850, and there was nothing in the past relations of the two divisions of the country to indicate that the same would not continue,—none could foresee how long.

Fortunately, the South grew impatient of this sure progress of gain, and wanted to grasp all at once, and then our eyes were forcibly opened, and we saw our past error, and redeemed it. The South found that *the wrath of the patient man*, which wisdom had ever advised the world to avoid, was terrible and destructive.

If we had resisted in the beginning, or at any subsequent occasion, the South would have threatened, scolded, and stormed, and there it would have ended. But perhaps the opportunity of extinguishing slavery would not have been offered, and we might have had it even to this day.

Perhaps it was best as it happened. The course of Providence is always the best.

Do you know how Judge Wilmot happened to have his name attached to the celebrated "Proviso" against the extension of slavery? General Garfield told me the story

When one of the Southern plans was before Congress, there were fourteen Democrats in the House who were determined to put this condition into the bill. They had hitherto gone with their party in favor of all the Southern demands. Now they prepared this proviso, and each one had a copy in his hands. They agreed that, at the proper time, all of them should rise (with probably many others), and call out, "Mr. Speaker," with the reasonable expectation that the Speaker would notice and acknowledge one of the fourteen. Wilmot caught the Speaker's eye, and offered the proviso, which went thereafter in his name. Judge Wilmot deserved the credit no more than any other of the fourteen; and how slight a turn of the Speaker's eye might have given the proviso another name?

Very truly and affectionately,
EDWARD JARVIS.

SAMUEL DOWNER, Esq., Boston.

LETTER FROM REV. JAMES FREEMAN CLARKE.

MAGNOLIA, MASS.

DEAR MR. DOWNER:—I have manifested my interest in the meeting of Free-Soilers already in two ways, unknown to you. I wrote a poem, to be read on that occasion, and wrote it amid the heats of summer and the idleness of vacation; thus, as the poet Saadi says, "Squeezing the moisture from a shrivelled brain, and digesting the smoke of a profitless lamp." This was one proof of my interest in your meeting. The second was, that when I came to the Landing, I did not disclose the fact that I had written these verses, and so spared you and the company the hearing of them. And now I give another proof of my unwillingness to be left out of your sympathies, by sending these poor lines, which you are at liberty to print or suppress, at your convenience.

Gratefully and sincerely yours,
JAMES FREEMAN CLARKE.

THERMOPYLÆ AND SALAMIS.

"Free Soil! Free Speech! Free Presses! and Free Men!"
Such were the watchwords on our standards, when
   We stood in Freedom's stern Thermopylæ,
And saw the vast barbaric host combine
To crush our thin but unretreating line,
   And plant, on innocent soil, the weed of Slavery.

Around us, and behind us, and before,
From Western prairie to the Atlantic shore,
   That Persian army stretched across the land;
It seemed the darkest hour of human fate,
For all the powers which govern Church and State,
With pride, and strength, and victory elate,
   Misleading or misled, made up the mighty band.

To drown our voice, old hates suspend their war;
The two great parties cease their endless jar,
   And, to appal our soul with strange surprises,
Calhoun and Webster walk one common way,
Like lamb and lion, who together play,
Led by that little child, called Henry Clay,—
   To save the Constitution's compromises.

Commerce and trade, behind them, shout aloud;
To Union meetings Wall and State street crowd;
   Mob, press, and parlor join the mighty throng;
Each subtle lawyer brings his precedent;
Each South-side doctor his cold argument;
And even the holy law of God is bent,
   To prove that black is white, and right is wrong.

What was our strength in that unequal fight?
Who stood with us to battle for the right,
   In that dread pass, our land's Thermopylæ?
Conscience—strong-siding champion—was there,
And God's eternal laws, like angels fair,
A heavenly army in the upper air,
   Prophets of hope and coming victory.

And hearts below, as brave as ever beat,
Which had no sense for failure or defeat,—
   Adams and Palfrey, Birney, Giddings, Hale,—
Soldiers made strong by danger and distress;
Heroes in street or Senate, Church or Press,
Like voices crying in the wilderness;
   Pilots, to guide the ship through breakers, night, and gale.

Through this Thermopylæ our land has passed,
And reached its glorious SALAMIS at last,
   When every slave is free, and all the land is one.
And now, when this dark cloud has passed away,
This night has settled into sunny day,
And we, on Slavery's tomb, keep holy day,
   Forget not those with whom the strife begun.

ADDRESS OF J. B. MANN OF NATICK.

Mr. PRESIDENT:—Our meeting to-day is not for the purpose of celebrating the first political anti-slavery movement made in this country, as seems to be the impression of our friend Mr. Tuck, who certainly did important work in New Hampshire a little earlier, but to take note of the anniversary of the Buffalo Convention, its preliminaries, and revive memories and associations of the noted year, 1848, when the anti-slavery sentiment of the country at large first crystallized into a formidable political national party.

But, leaving this, allow me to say one word by way of reminiscence. Our distinguished Senator, Mr. Hoar, has done justice to the memory of Charles Allen, the delegate to the Whig National Convention which nominated General Taylor, who had the courage to pronounce the party dead from that moment, and take his hat, and, in company with Henry Wilson, march out of the convention. While he has not intended to depreciate Mr. Wilson, I am sure the effect of his remarks leaves an impression that Allen was the leader and Wilson the follower,—not only in the sense that he went out of the hall last, but that he went at the suggestion, or under the inspiration, of Judge Allen as a leader. This was not so. The idea of bolting was planned in Boston, and was well understood by several before the delegates started for Philadelphia. I well remember that Wilson was fully determined not to abide the nomination of General Taylor, unless something authentic came from Taylor himself at the convention, which could be accepted by the believers in the "Wilmot Proviso"; and he was active and untiring in his efforts to bring the whole delegation up to his views, though, I suppose, Allen was in accord with him.

These movements attracted the attention of a gentleman, well known and held in esteem in Boston at that time, by the name of Daniel Webster, and he invited Allen and Wilson to a conference at the Tremont House, which was held the week before the convention, and attended by several other prominent men. I saw Wilson early the next day, and he was in high spirits. Webster, he said, indorsed the plan of adhering to the "Wilmot Proviso" as a finality, or to the idea of the ordinance of '87, and would support them in insisting upon it, and having the candidate committed to it.

It was supposed that a majority of the Massachusetts delegates were in the Webster interest, and could be controlled by him to follow the plan agreed upon; but, as it happened, Allen and Wilson had to march out by themselves, exciting derision as a "county judge, and a contemptible cobbler," striving to smash a machine that was about to run over them. To break the Webster phalanx in Massachusetts, Abbot Lawrence had been tickled with the promise of support as the candidate for Vice-President on the ticket with Taylor, and having for many years done not a little in behalf of Mr. Webster, he now took very kindly to the idea that it was a good time to do something for himself; and then it would be a great consolation to Massachusetts to have the Vice-Presidency, in case the Presidency was not to fall to her lot, after the battle was over. Fillmore was tickled with the other end of the same straw, and that was the straw which broke the back of Daniel Webster, and made General Taylor President of the United States.

Upon the return of Allen and Wilson, the Worcester Convention was organized, and with the concurrence of Mr. Webster; but subsequently he gave way, and supported General Taylor—as candidate never was supported before—by declaring to the amazed countenance of Abbot Lawrence and others, who paid for the Marshfield speech, that it was a "nomination not fit to be made."

Well, at Worcester we had Sumner, Allen, Samuel Hoar, Hale, Giddings, Lew Campbell, Hopkins, Wilson, and others too numerous to name. It was a stirring time. I had never seen masses of men so moved as they were upon this occasion, and except in connection with the scenes of the great Rebellion, I have never seen them so moved since. We are able to measure now the meaning of what was in the souls of the men of that day, though very few of us know the half of what it cost in study, effort, zeal, and unflinching courage and perseverance, to bring about the final result. To the organizing brain, the settled purpose, the sagacious counsel, the strong faith, the unyielding tenacity, and constant fidelity of Henry Wilson, more, I think, was due than to any single person in shaping the course of the Free-Soil party, and in making finally true the declaration of Charles Allen at Philadelphia, "The Whig party is no more, and will have no resurrection." He performed a work no other man of our time was qualified to perform. Other men contributed eloquence, thought, inspiration, counsel, labor, faith, and gave of their time and wealth, and voice and brain, to push along the great work. But Wilson gave himself. He lost all thought or care for money, and business, and ease, and convenience, and sleep, and bodily health, and social enjoyment, and went in, with all he had and all he hoped for, to aid the cause .This was what was needed, and what, in a large measure, no other man gave, or had to give.

I would not say here or anywhere that Wilson was not ambitious, for he was,—intensely ambitious; but that does not detract from his merit as a worker, and a producer of results. To succeed, Emerson says, "hitch your chariot to the stars"; and Wilson, fastening his to the glorious star of right, found, and deserved, the gratification of a laudable ambition. This occasion should not pass without at least so much of acknowledgment to the memory of one of the most useful practical statesmen of the stirring times through which we have in the last thirty years been passing, and who was the personal acquaintance, probably, of every man within the sound of my voice.

ADDRESS OF J. E. CRANE OF BRIDGEWATER.

We stand here to-day to revive early memories of the party that was specially organized to reclaim this Government from the grasp of slavery. The men who were foremost in that movement were resolute and strong to maintain a righteous cause, regardless of threats, intimidations, or proscription.

It was a happy conception of Mr. Downer to call the survivors of that early contest to this charming spot, to recount their trials and their victories, and to rejoice together in the retrospect of the receding past. With joy we greet each other; with delight we grasp the hand of fraternal friendship. With so much to review that is cheering, and with such happy memories as press upon us, there is still a tinge of sadness as we note the absent ones, whom the Great Reaper has gathered to their rewards.

Sumner, Wilson, Allen, Mann, Phillips, Burlingame, Howe, Andrew, Webb, and others, " of whom the world was not worthy," whose voices inspired our early convocations for the cause of freedom, are with us in spirit, and to their memories would we devote our most fragrant and unfading garlands.

The Old Colony was represented in that early struggle by many of whose worth it would be well to speak, who have passed away, but who still live in the memory and affections of those who knew them best. Tillinghast, the distinguished teacher of Bridgewater; Davis, the young and able son of the Pilgrims; Philo Leach, Joseph Kingman, and Dr. Caleb Swan,—all ardently devoted to the high duty of reclaiming the country from the stain of oppression. May we not rejoice with thanksgiving to the Great Author of all for what our eyes have been permitted to behold, while others who desired it long, died without the sight? Assembled as we are, not for self-gratulations, but to mark the historic past, and to do homage to those who have gone before, may we not catch a new inspiration to higher and better aims, and pledge with true and honest hearts the remnant of our days to unfaltering devotion to the best interest of our beloved Commonwealth, and our common country?

ADDRESS OF REV. EDWIN THOMPSON OF WALPOLE, MASS.

Mr. CHAIRMAN:—I noticed that the Hon. George F. Hoar said he did not know but he was too young to claim much connection with the Free-Soil movement. His remark has suggested the thought to me, that, perhaps, I am too old, having been connected with the anti-slavery movement from the start,—somewhere about 1828 or 1829. I had given some five hundred addresses on the subject previous to the organization of the Free-Soil party. I happened to be present when the Liberty party, with which I voted, united with the Free-Soil party; and, if my memory does not fail me, the Hon. William Jackson—a name never to be forgotten, certainly one of the best men whom I ever knew—presided at the last meeting of the Liberty party, which was held in Tremont Temple. I remember, after the Free-Soil party was organized, that, in connection with my friend, F. W. Bird, I labored to unite our forces with those of such Democrats as were more in favor of freedom than of the mere name of Democracy, in order to secure the election of some true man and friend of freedom, who would more truly represent the great heart of Massachusetts in the Senate than he who had recently so disgraced it. I remember that Mr. Bird and myself visited quite a number of towns with this purpose in view. Mr. Bird agreed to find horse and carriage, and to go with me when his business would permit. As Mr. Bird has remarked in his speech to-day, we must have all been somewhat disinterested, as we never took any pay for time or services. Of course, neither Mr. Bird nor myself, at that time, ever expected to obtain any public office by the course we were pursuing. We visited other counties besides our own, to awaken the people in reference to the matter. I remember that the "Boston Atlas" said, in the report of a meeting where the forces of the Democrats and Free-Soilers united, that "two jockeys from Norfolk County were present," meaning, of course, Mr. Bird and myself. We succeeded in bringing about what we desired; viz., a union of the two parties. These labors, in connection with those of others in different parts of the State, resulted, by the aid of Divine Providence, in the election of Charles Sumner to the United States Senate. I have always felt grateful that I was able to contribute to so glorious a result. I thought then, and I think now, that the course of yourself, Mr. Chairman, on that occasion, was perfectly sublime; and, however different our opinions may be now, I believe that that course, at that time,—the son of John Quincy Adams, with your surroundings, and your prospects for the future,—was, in its noble self-sacrifice, second to that of no other man in the Commonwealth. Time would fail me to speak of our noble friends of the past, such as Judge Allen, Hon. Robert Rantoul, Jr., Hon. Horace Mann, of whom our friend, Mr. Downer, has spoken so justly, Rev. Charles T. Torrey,

Hon. Henry Wilson, Hon. Samuel Hoar, Hon. Amasa Walker, John W. Browne, with many others, who gave their hearts and hands to this movement, which, in connection with the earlier anti-slavery agitation, and with the aid of other events, unlooked for by us, but, as we trust, not unforeseen in the providence of God, has resulted in the liberation of four millions of human beings from a worse than Egyptian bondage.

ADDRESS OF ALBERT TOLMAN OF WORCESTER.

Mr. PRESIDENT:—The reference by Mr. Hoar to the meeting held at Worcester to give Judge Allen an opportunity to report his doings at the Philadelphia Convention revives many recollections. Our friend, Mr. Chamberlin, who is one of your guests, remembers the doubts and discouragements experienced at the time. He met Mr. Allen immediately after his return, and assured him, if he would speak, he would be sustained by a large number of respectable citizens; but that, on the part of gentlemen of his own and other professions, there might be coldness for a time.

Then, as always, before and since, Worcester was the home of professional gentlemen of superior ability, many of whom, as you well know, sir, have done the State and country good service; none of them much harm, and so all are to be gratefully remembered.

Then there was another element in the population of Worcester. For twenty years it had increased rapidly, by the coming in of persons from the surrounding towns to engage in various productive pursuits; and whether they were to be employers or employés, they were equals, and the Worcester of that day had come to be called the paradise of mechanics. In this emergency they were reliable. We fear its growth since, and the increase of our other towns, has not been quite so healthy. There were trials about that first meeting; many thought it would be a failure—only a fizzle. But the large hall was crowded; numbers were there to scoff, not to listen; but they did listen; some repented, some resolved again. Our honorable Senator has just given us his estimate of the speech Charles Allen delivered that evening. Most of us remember it. And when, at its close, the Rev. George Allen came to the platform, and in clear, ringing tones gave forth the sentiment that was repeated with enthusiasm at so many of the meetings afterwards, "Massachusetts wears no chains and spurns all bribes; she goes now, and ever will go, for free thought and free speech, free soil and free men," the Free-Soil party was born in strength, with its distinctive name.

Worcester, at its next election, made Henry Chapin mayor. Nearly all the representatives from Worcester County were Free-Soilers, and Charles Allen was elected to Congress from his district.

ADDRESS OF THE HON. SEBEAS C. MAINE.

Mr. PRESIDENT, AND GENTLEMEN OF THE OLD FREE-SOIL PARTY:—
It is with feelings of deep emotion that I look upon this assembly, —those upturned faces, beneath bald or thinly covered heads,—remembering as I do that but yesterday you were in the full strength and beauty of manly vigor, having espoused a cause but one step less distasteful to political rule than the unpardonable sin of Abolition. In fact, I see before me while I speak some of that "accursed race," who dared to question the right of property in another by reason of caste or color; and if I may be pardoned for personalities, I must say to our worthy and venerable friend who has spread out this bountiful feast for our enjoyment, Thou art one of them, "for thy speech betrayeth thee."

There are volumes in two words in the heading of the call for this interesting meeting,—"*Then*" and "*Now*." How few, alas! of that little band of determined men are here to-day to answer to the roll-call! We seek them and their places in vain. The invisible shuts them out; and yet we feel, we know, that to-day they are here present with us.

> "How cheering the thought that the spirits in bliss
> May bow their bright wings to a world such as this."

Among the many who "have gone over the river," and who have been alluded to this day with so much kind remembrance, foremost in my recollection is the name of Stephen C. Phillips. I was called to preside over the first Free-Soil convention held in the old Fifth Congressional District at Salem. Mr. Phillips was chairman of the Committee on Resolutions. There are doubtless some here to-day who attended that convention. If so, they can bear testimony with me of his great earnestness on that occasion, and to the strength and significance of the resolutions by him presented. "Then" it required courage to be an Abolitionist, or even a Free-Soil man; but after a few years, it was apparent that the tide was setting in another direction, until at length the truth of the proverb was verified, "Whom the gods would destroy they first make mad." Rebellion came, and with it the great struggle for freedom for three millions of slaves,—a prophetic number indeed! The number of the Israelites that God released from Egyptian bondage;—the number of colonists that in our "grandfathers' days" scorned to be enslaved. A Moses was provided for the Israelites, a Washington for the colonists, and a Lincoln for the oppressed slaves. The labor of years was finished when, with his pen, he signed the proclamation of emancipation.

I hope we may never cease to wonder at the result of the signing of that proclamation. Three millions of slaves at once transformed to freemen, and three millions of voters for the first time discovered that they were Abolitionists, and had been from their earliest recollection, and were ready with overwhelming testimony to prove it! And now you, venerable gentlemen, who have "borne the burden and heat of the day," are continually reminded by those gentlemen of sudden and miraculous conversion of the great obligations you are under to them for bringing about the thing which, most of all, you desired! Oh, how much labor and anxiety would have been saved you, gentlemen, if those hidden fires of freedom, so long smouldering in those three million bosoms, had kindled into a flame thirty years sooner!

Our worthy host has interested us with some incidents in his early conversion to the cause of freedom. Pardon me for referring to my own. In 1836, while yet a stripling, I happened to be spending a few days in the quiet little village of Canistota, in Central New York. While I was there, the Abolitionists from various parts of the State met in convention at that place. They were attacked by a mob, their meeting broken up, and their printing-press thrown into the canal. Among those present was Gerrit Smith of Peterboro'. He was not there to take an active part in the convention, but only as "a looker-on in Vienna." When he saw the convention broken up, he extended to them an invitation to meet the next morning at Peterboro', where he promised them protection. His invitation was accepted, and at sunrise on the following morning the entire delegation set out on foot for Peterboro', distant seven miles. I was at Peterboro' when the delegation arrived, and entered the "meeting-house" with them. Mr. Smith was chosen by an unanimous vote to preside over their deliberations. Although many years have since passed by, still the doings of that day are as fresh in my mind as the doings of yesterday. And although I have since seen many a noble-looking man presiding on many occasions, I have never seen the equal of Gerrit Smith on that occasion; and his language was the perfection of human utterance.

He said that he attended the convention the day before as an interested listener, but the acts of an infuriated mob, and the meditations of a sleepless night, had made the path of duty plain before him in the future; "and from this hour," said he, with emotion, "my life, my property, and all I have, and all that I can do, shall be devoted to the cause of Abolition."

I know not how many were converted on that occasion, but I do know that one, at least, was converted. We have lived to see the great work accomplished, but no man can tell how it was done, and we leave it as a decree of fate!

"Whatever acts we perpetrate,
We only row,—we're steered by fate."

LETTER FROM ELIZUR WRIGHT.

[From the Boston Transcript of Aug. 13.]

TO THE EDITOR OF THE TRANSCRIPT:—The Free-Soil celebration at Downer's little paradise, Thursday, was every way a most delicious occasion, but there were two historical points that seemed to me not to have been brought out in their true or full light. They were slightly refracted. One was the cause of Henry Clay's defeat in 1844, and the other the reason for making Martin Van Buren the Free-Soil candidate in 1848. Had John G. Whittier been present, I think he could have given a clearer vision on both those points.

The earliest of the political Abolitionists were friends, and some of them almost worshippers, of Henry Clay. But soon after the formation of the American Anti-Slavery Society, in 1833, and years before political action was commenced, they entered into correspondence with Mr. Clay and some other Southern statesmen, both individually and collectively. The object was to discover their honest, inside opinions as to the ultimate freedom or destiny of the negro. Mr. Clay, I know very well, in letters marked "strictly confidential," responded to the letters of the Anti-Slavery Society in such a way as not only to extinguish all hope of any aid from him, but as to convince the executive committee that he was a more dangerous enemy to the freedom of the negro even than John C. Calhoun. His *words* for freedom had not been meant for American soil. I am very sure that Mr. Whittier's faith in him was so much shaken that he did not consider the election of Polk in 1844 a greater evil than that of Clay would have been. It was not Mr. Clay's letter to citizens of Alabama, or of "Western New York," that defeated him, but his hypocritical conduct years before, and especially his making himself the stiffest pillar of the slave power in the United States Senate, Feb. 7, 1839, when he said: "I know that there is a visionary dogma which holds that negro slaves cannot be the subjects of property. I shall not dwell long with this speculative abstraction. That is property which the law declares to be property. Two hundred years of legislation have sanctioned and sanctified negro slaves as property."

Here was the reason why 70,000 men voted for Birney, and elected Polk. Many more would have done so, probably, if the Whigs in their blind madness had not forged a letter from Birney to Garland, in which the Liberty candidate was made, just before election, to sell himself to the Democrats for a seat in the Michigan Legislature. That cruel and infamous forgery was so well calculated to deceive, that no less a man than Daniel Webster backed its genuineness by the "fool's argument" of a bet!

Yet even the most conscientious of the Whigs, including probably many of those who went into the Free-Soil movement of 1848, have hardly yet forgiven the Abolitionists for voting for Birney in 1844. They seem inclined to put it into history that the increase of the anti-slavery vote from 70,000 in 1844 to 300,000 in 1848 was pretty much their work.

This brings me to the second point, why was Van Buren and not McLean the candidate of the Buffalo Convention? And it is here that Mr. Adams and the whole clam-bake, it seems to me, fail to do justice to history. Mr. McLean was a distinguished Whig citizen, whose position in regard to slavery was almost wholly unknown.

With all Liberty men, a part of whom had already nominated Gerrit Smith, his nomination at Buffalo would have fallen pretty dead. Mr. Van Buren, who had incurred the displeasure of the then extant Abolitionists in 1836 by his foolish campaign pledge to veto abolition in the District of Columbia, had, while President, been rather discreet on the subject of slavery, except perhaps, in regard to the Amistad captives, so bravely rescued at last by John Quincy Adams. In his last message, he put some paragraphs about the African slave trade, which, though they did not count much with the Abolitionists at the time, cost him, as he must have been conscious they would, some slaveholding votes; for the Gulf slaveholders were then not only coveting Texas, but looking for cheaper slaves than the "vigintial crops" of Maryland and Virginia. He had been already nominated for his second term, and had he been the mere trickster the Whigs represented him, would have been elected. But in doughfacing, the other party had got the inside track, and Van Buren went down before "Harrison and Hard Cider." In the whirl-wind, hurricane, and tornado of that campaign, the Abolitionists, though the male members of their societies exceeded fifty thousand, could rally only seven thousand votes for James G. Birney. Even the colored voters of Ward 6 went with the Whigs in mass, voting for Harrison only to be snubbed by Mayor Chapman and Marshal Josiah Quincy, Jr., at his public funeral, to which they had invited *all* citizens.

The Democratic party, especially the Northern part of it, was intent upon nominating Martin Van Buren in 1844, and the more so from his defeat in 1840, which was regarded by them as undeserved, and which certainly was so in relation to his successful rival. That Mr. Van Buren could have secured the nomination of his party, and, of course, an election, by simply remaining silent, or writing a letter in his characteristic style, no observer of the period can doubt.

Instead of that, in March, 1844, he wrote a letter to a Mr. Hammet, in which he not only took ground against the annexation of Texas, but gave the reasons for it in the most admirable and overwhelming manner. For once, at least, he put meaning into his language. He deliberately threw away the chance of his nomination by any pro-slavery party. It may well be doubted whether, considering all the circumstances, a more heroic act has been recorded of any American statesman. Mr. Clay, who, as a party man in quest of a nomination, had nothing to lose and everything to gain by it, wrote a similar, though shorter letter, about the same time. He secured the nomination, and then, to secure votes at the South, favored annexation, or, as Mr. Adams says, equivocated.

The principal leaders of the Liberty party, who had defeated Clay in 1844, were not so stupid as to forget, in 1848, Van Buren's letter to Hammet in 1844. They wanted no new letter after that, only to know if he would consent to the nomination. When he was nominated and did accept, they threw up their caps for him with a will, as the following extract from John G. Whittier in the "National Era" will show; and, what is more, it will show where the change of heart probably came from which Mr. Van Buren had experienced since 1836. Says Mr. Whittier:—

"There is one circumstance, in this connection, which we have always regarded as highly honorable to Martin Van Buren. On the appearance of the message containing the Veto Pledge, one prominent Democrat, faithful among the faithless, condemned it boldly, unreservedly, and administered to its author an indignant rebuke. This man was William Leggett. Two years after, that brilliant and heroic genius, broken down by protracted illness, was advised to seek relief in a more genial climate, but his pecuniary circumstances were such as to preclude the idea of his profiting by this advice. It was at this time that President Van Buren tendered to him the honorable post of the mission to Guatemala, thus evincing his superiority to merely personal resentment, and his magnanimous appreciation of honesty and fidelity to principle, even when exercised at his own expense, and contrary to his own views of expediency. He knew Leggett to be honest; he knew him to be a true Democrat; and in the season of his sickness and poverty, he visited him with a testimonial of confidence and esteem, which was as grateful to its recipient as it was creditable to the head and heart of the bestower.

"We turn from that dark season, when both the great political parties felt themselves compelled to offer obeisance to the slave power, with joy and hope to the bright promise of the present time. We opposed Van Buren in 1837 because, and only because, he occupied a wrong position as respects slavery. He has now set himself right before the country and the world. He has rescued the honored name of Democracy from the reproach of an alliance with slavery. We can hesitate no longer. We cast to the winds our old prejudices and misgivings, and cheerfully, heartily, give our assent to the action of the Buffalo Convention."

The speakers, at the commemoration festival, seemed almost as good at forgetting as remembering. Even Mr. Tuck, in his anxiety to remember our genial John P. Hale as the first anti-slavery United States Senator, forgot that Thomas Morris, the Liberty-party candidate for Vice-President, had done good anti-slavery work in the Senate still earlier. It was fortunate for the Buffalo Convention of August 9, 1848, that it had in it a good sprinkling of Liberty-party men like Joshua Leavitt, who looked for honest *men* in all parties, and who remembered that it was William Leggett, a young Democratic editor, who, with the aid of Charles King, an editor of the old Federalist type, rescued the American Anti-Slavery Society from the mobs set upon it in 1834 by that prince of Whig editors, James Watson Webb. The good die young, and so died many who in the days of danger did more to free the slave than any now living.

ELIZUR WRIGHT.

AUGUST 11, 1877.

APPENDIX.

LETTER FROM THE HON. CHARLES A. PHELPS.

BOSTON, August 3, 1877.

SAMUEL DOWNER, Esq.

DEAR SIR:—I am greatly obliged to you for your kind invitation to the "Reunion of the Free-Soilers of 1848," on the 9th of August, and deeply regret that it will not be in my power to be present. Many of the leaders in that great movement, Wilson, Sumner, Burlingame, Phillips, have passed on; others, advanced in years,—

> "Walk thoughtful
> On the silent, solemn shore
> Of that vast ocean
> We must sail so soon."

It will be a day of reminiscences of the living and the dead. You will, perhaps, pardon me for contributing a few of my own memories.

My first recollection of the great anti-slavery struggle began in 1831, in visits, as a boy of ten years of age, to the office of the "Liberator," where William Lloyd Garrison and Isaac Knapp set up the types with their own hands, living on bread and milk, and sleeping in berths in one corner of the office. There they "fired the shot heard round the world." The office was in Merchant's Hall, at the corner of Congress and Water Streets, where the Shawmut Bank now stands. The paper was started without subscribers and continued without capital. I may be excused for remembering that an honored father, now no more, was one of the little band of twelve or fifteen persons who, in January, 1832, formed the New England Anti-Slavery Society. In 1833, Mr. Garrison went to England and labored with Wilberforce, Macaulay, and other English abolitionists, in the struggle for West India Emancipation. When about to return to America, they expressed their gratitude and said, "Now, what can we do for you?" he replied, "Send us George Thompson." There must be some present at your meeting who remember the man and his eloquent appeals. The anti-slavery sentiment in the Northern States was greatly increased and strengthened by his fervid oratory. Lord Brougham said of him in England: "I rise to take the crown of this glorious victory of emancipation from every other head, and place it upon George Thompson." His meetings in Boston were generally held in Julian Hall, at the corner of Congress and Water streets, almost the only hall open in those days to the despised abolitionists. I attended most of his meetings, to the sad neglect of my school lessons. I can see and hear him now! He was a natural orator, a tall, spare man, having the proverbial large mouth given to all great orators and singers. He had a sonorous voice and an animated delivery. His face resembled somewhat the face of Rev. Joseph Cook. His mouth, when open, recalled the story of the dentist who told his patient that it was "needless to open his mouth any wider, as he should stand on the outside." He lectured in most of the large towns and cities of New England. He was a man of gentle manners, of the loftiest courage, and of indomitable will. He was fearless of the mobs which so often greeted him, and was unsparing in denunciation of the crimes of slavery.

The fierce hatred of the unwelcome truths of anti-slavery culminated in the Garrison mob in Boston, October 21, 1835. The Anti-Slavery office was then in the third story of the building now numbered 180 Washington Street. In front of the building was a large sign lettered "Anti-Slavery Office." The crowd began to assemble about 3 o'clock in the afternoon, with threats and shouts. They dispersed a meeting of ladies in the hall. Soon after, men appeared at the windows with hammers, took down the sign, lowered it with ropes to the sidewalk, amid yells and shouts, where it was received by five or six well-known citizens (I never forgot their faces, or even their dress), and it was soon broken in pieces. With the privilege of a boy, I rushed in and saved a good-sized relic. The next day, on showing it to Mr. Benjamin F. Hallett, he said, "Keep it for years; it is a piece of history," and, calling for a pen, he wrote a glowing inscription on the wood.

Hearing that Mr. Garrison was in the rear of his office, I went around to Wilson's Lane, where, soon after, he appeared at the second-story window of a carpenter's shop, the mob shouting to those near to force him to come down. As he stepped upon the ladder to descend, his hat off, his spectacles removed, his face untroubled, he said, quietly, "I shall go down unresisting. Hail Columbia, land of liberty." As soon as he reached the yard, he was seized, led up Wilson's Lane, surrounded by a crowd which filled the street, and with a man on each side holding him by the collar of his coat. As they turned into State Street, there were shouts, "Tar and feather him," "To the pump, to the pump," which then stood at the east end of the Old State House. But the crowd surged on up the north side of the Old State House, then the City Hall. When opposite the north door, several city officials,—among them I remember the portly form of

Deacon Samuel Greeley,—rushed into the street, seized Garrison, and carried him into the building. Soon a hack drove up, and Mr. Garrison appeared with an overcoat and sealskin cap; he was hurried into the carriage and driven to the Leveret Street jail for safe-keeping. Like all other mobs, it was a cowardly mob. Not more than a dozen men did the disgraceful work, and fifty determined policemen would have scattered the whole crowd. But it is along such a highway, marked every furlong by scaffolds and gibbets and prisons, that Truth has marched to her grandest conquests. In 1837, I had an opportunity to witness, for the first time, the methods of calling a Faneuil Hall meeting. The city government had refused the use of the hall to the Rev. Dr. Channing and others, to denounce the murder of Lovejoy. I heard my father remark to a friend, "The refusal of Faneuil Hall for a meeting to denounce mob law is a disgrace to Boston. We ought to have a meeting to resent such an outrage." In a few moments, I was told to make copies of a call for a meeting in the Old City Hall, and was sent out to the newspapers with the notices. The meeting was held, Faneuil Hall secured, and I shall never forget the surprise and delight with which the brilliant first speech of Wendell Phillips, then twenty-six years old, was received in defence of the objects of the meeting. My acquaintance with Charles Sumner began in my boyhood, when he was a student at Cambridge. In 1846, in a little convention of Anti-Slavery men, assembled in the piano warerooms of Dea. Timothy Gilbert, I had the honor of nominating Mr. Sumner as a candidate for Congress from the Boston District, and was both astonished and pleased at receiving a call from him the next evening, to thank me for what he graciously called a speech. The Free-Soil movement of 1848, then called by its opponents a "fizzle," heralded the dissolution of the great Whig and Democratic parties. It was accelerated by Mr. Webster's speech on the 7th March, 1850, and fully accomplished by the repeal of the Missouri Compromise in 1854. What a retrospect! From the little obscure office of the "Liberator," the uprising of the loyal millions in 1861, the emancipation of a race, and the regeneration of the Republic! The lesson which the Free-Soil movement teaches to young men, is, that moral truth is invincible; no party organization can resist its power. Have the courage of your opinions. Go forth to the people for their verdict.

> "A good cause will stand and will abide,
> Legions of angels fight upon its side."

I am, very truly yours,

CHARLES A. PHELPS.

SAMUEL DOWNER, Esq.

Reunion of Free-Soilers of 1848.

LETTER FROM JAMES A. BRIGGS, Esq.

54 East 25th Street, New York,
August 6, 1877.

My Dear Sir:—Many thanks for your invitation to attend a Reunion of the Free-Soilers of 1848, at Melville Garden, on the 9th of August, instant. I very much regret that official engagements will deprive me of the pleasure of being at the Reunion, and of "crossing palms" with some of the men who were engaged in that "bloodless victory," in that ever-memorable year.

Many who were with us in that great contest, and bore themselves nobly and well in its important work, have "passed through the dark waters," "to the beautiful land," to receive the reward of well-doing here in this lower life.

Eighteen hundred and forty-eight was an eventful year for this country, and no political convention ever held was more important and far-reaching in its influence for human freedom than the Free-Soil Convention at Buffalo, in August, 1848. It was the first convention that ever placed obstructions on the track of slavery, that the skilful engineers of that system of wrong had not the ability and power to remove. That convention was careful to act within the Constitution on the slave question, and at the same time it was determined that no power, unknown to the Constitution, should be used for the purpose of extending slavery into new territory, where slavery was unknown. The late Judge McLean said to me, in a letter written in July, 1848, "That Congress had no more right to make a slave than it had to make a king"; and this was the key-note of that convention.

What memories crowd upon the mind at the recollection of that magnificent assemblage of men, who had met for one common purpose, moved by one common thought, actuated by one common feeling, and who had left their former political parties and associations, determined upon one thing, and one only,—to prevent the extension of human slavery!

Mr. Charles Francis Adams was the president of that convention, able and accomplished, a representative of the culture and refinement and learning of the East. And there was Samuel Lewis of Ohio, the first Commissioner of Education in Ohio,—" the eldest born of the daughters of the Ordinance of 1787,"—whose alma mater was a Cincinnati brick-yard, but whose natural, effective, magnetic eloquence moved the hearts of men, as the strong winds move the dried leaves of autumn, and whose burning words for "the rights of man" will ever be remembered by all who ever listened to them. And there was one of your strongest men, in whose reach were all the high places of honor *your* people hold within their gift, Mr. Stephen C. Phillips, who had come to Buffalo with all the ardor of a knight of the olden time, and with high and holy purpose to do battle for "the right." I see now his commanding form, his kingly presence, his noble face, his eyes kindling with the enthusiasm of his great soul, as he stood before the assembled thousands on the last evening of that convention, and closed his magnificent speech with these words, "Let your rallying cry be, Van Buren and Free-Soil, Adams and Liberty."

And there was Mr. Benjamin F. Butler, the Attorney-General of the United States, the long-time personal and political friend of Mr. Van Buren, one of the most accomplished and elegant men in the land, who had come to help "crush out" General Cass, whose opinions were as shifting as the wind, and who had been successful in throwing overboard, from the old Democratic ship, Mr. Van Buren, who was saved on a Free-Soil plank, and, on that plank, wrecked General Cass and the Democratic party in November, 1848. Mr. Butler's elegance was in strong contrast with the sturdy vigor and homely strength of Mr. Joshua R. Giddings, who had won more victories in "the House" over slavery than any man, save Mr. John Quincy Adams, and who was as cordially hated as any man in all the land for his persistent opposition to slavery and every attempt to extend it.

And there, too, in that assembly of notable men, was one central and commanding person, "the observed of all observers"; a man who had never held high office, nor any office, save that of a Councilman of his ward in the Common Council in the city of Cincinnati, Salmon P. Chase. His was the master-mind in framing the resolves of that convention. When he came forward to the platform, and announced, as chairman of the Committee on Resolutions, that a report had been unanimously agreed upon, and read the resolutions, the whole audience stood upon their feet, shout after shout went up, and hats were thrown to the ceiling, and all jealousy and distrust were gone, and men felt like brothers who were all engaged in one common cause.

Other men were there who had made their mark, and who were known to fame, and others who have since become known to fame.

"The Barn Burners," as the Free-Soil Democrats of New York were known, came there determined to avenge the slaughter of the favorite son of New York, Mr. Van Buren. On the morning of the day the nominations were made, there were a number of Buckeyes stopping at the Mansion House,—Messrs. Chase, Bolton, Giddings, etc.,—when Mr. Benjamin F. Butler, Mr. George Rathbone, Mr. Martin Grover, and one other, who was a member of Congress, whose name I cannot recall, came to where we were sitting, and Mr. Butler said to us: "Gentlemen, there are two things that can be done here to-day. Nominate Judge McLean, and General Cass will be President of the United States. Nominate Mr. Van Buren, and General Taylor will be elected; for we can assure you, that with Mr. Van Buren as a candidate, the contest in New York will be between General Taylor and Mr. Van Buren. General Cass 'is a dead cock in the pit.' Now, if you prefer the election of an honest old soldier, like General Taylor, to the election of a dough-face like General Cass, nominate Mr. Van Buren." We were in telegraphic communication with Judge McLean. He would not accept the second place on the ticket, and said "he thought the nomination for President belonged to Mr. Van Buren." The convention assembled. The platform of principles was satisfactory. Mr. Van Buren was nominated for President, and Mr. Charles Francis Adams for Vice-President. These nominations resulted in the election of General Taylor and Mr. Fillmore, and saved California and New Mexico to free labor, and put an end forever to the extension of slavery on American soil. Thenceforth there was free soil for free men! The Buffalo Convention of August, 1848, saved an empire to freedom. He who bore a part in the work of that convention may well feel that he has not lived in vain. Many who were there lived to see "the giant curse removed." Others passed away, and could only see the fruits of their labor from the "far-distant shore."

The Free-Soil movement of 1848 put Mr. Chase into the Senate of the United States from Ohio, and Mr. Charles Sumner into the United States Senate from Massachusetts.

I met, for the first time, Mr. Sumner, in Buffalo, the day before the convention. I told him "there were 3,000 Buckeyes in Buffalo who wished to hear him speak, and they would call him out to-morrow." Putting out both of his hands, he replied, "I cannot speak, I cannot speak." I repeated, "We shall call you out to-morrow." The morrow came. I went up to "The American," asked for Mr. Sumner, and was told by a gentleman from Massachusetts that Mr. Sumner had left the city and gone to Niagara Falls. I repeated what I had said to Mr. Sumner the day before, and was told that Mr. Sumner probably was not prepared with a speech; and then asked if he was one of those Eastern men who could not speak unless his speech was carefully written out and committed? The answer was, "Yes." Mr. Sumner did not return to the Buffalo Convention, and, of course, took no part in the work of that meeting. Why, I do not know. A new field was to be opened; new work was to be engaged in; the hopes of men were to be realized or blighted, and ambitions to be satisfied or wrecked. He was a noble worker in after days. The victory for which we hoped in 1848 was afterwards won. God grant that in all our land there may be peace, abundant prosperity, and a just recognition by each of the rights of all! May we ever acknowledge this great truth, that God has so linked us together in this wonderful chain of being, that an injury done to one person is an injury to all, and, sooner or later, the race must pay the penalty of the violated law!

The world moves, and the hands on the dial-plate of the face of Time point to Universal Freedom, to Universal Education, and, I hope, "in the good time coming," to Universal Temperance among men, and to faith in God.

Yours truly,

JAMES A. BRIGGS.

Mr. SAMUEL DOWNER, Boston, Mass.

LETTER FROM THE HON. M. M. FISHER.

MEDWAY, August 7, 1877.

SAMUEL DOWNER, Esq.

DEAR SIR:—Through inadvertence, I had forgotten to reply, as requested, to your kind invitation to attend the Reunion of the Free-Soilers of 1848.

I have, I assure you, anticipated a very pleasant meeting on that occasion, especially with such of the representative delegates to the Buffalo Convention, now living, as may be present.

I am glad to see that Mr. Adams, who, with Mr. William J. Reynolds, now dead, was associated with me as delegates from Norfolk, is called to preside.

Since receiving your note, I have lived much in the past, and reviewed my personal relation to many things connected with the early progress of the anti-slavery cause. In thought I have again attended the *first* anniversary of the American Anti-Slavery Society as delegate, in 1833, and gone South, visited the *slave pens* in Washington, and distributed *tracts* and *books* to *slaveholders*.

Have again delivered, in Amherst College, the *first* essay on this question, in 1833. Gone over all the towns in Norfolk County, from 1840 to 1848, to establish the Liberty party.

Have read over the first petition to the great American Missionary Board on this subject, at Worcester, in 1845. I feel that I can say, in this matter, as old Æneas says about the destruction of Troy, "All of which I saw, and part of which I was."

I trust that a roll will be made up of those who attend this Reunion, and measures adopted to reassemble at some future time, if not at a regular period, "to count over the battles fought in freedom's cause."

Yours respectfully,

M. M. FISHER.

LETTER FROM HON. THOMAS RUSSELL.

BOSTON, August 8, 1877.

DEAR SIR:—I regret that I cannot join your goodly company to-morrow. It was not altogether pleasant to be a Free-Soiler in 1848. It is very pleasant now to have been one. It is a certificate of political good character—for the past. It is also an assurance to ourselves. You know the familiar story of Cromwell's death-bed, when he asked his minister whether he was sure about the final perseverance of the saints. "Certainly," said he. "Then," said Cromwell, "I am safe. I know I was once in a state of grace." The Free-Soiler of '48, whatever his wanderings have been since, feels that he was once in a state of grace.

One recollection of those times. We young speakers were fond of personality, but in those days of rapid progress I found that the men whom we were assailing were constantly placing themselves by our side,—a good reason for giving up the practice of harsh speaking. So it has been since. Still the world moves fast; still—

"Our frowning foemen of the night
Are brothers at the dawn of day."

With all good wishes, I am
Yours, very truly,

THOMAS RUSSELL.

S. DOWNER, Esq.

LETTER FROM THE HON. WILLIAM B. SPOONER.

PETERSHAM, August 4, 1877.

SAMUEL DOWNER, Esq.

MY DEAR SIR:—I am very much obliged for the invitation to meet the "Free-Soilers of 1848," and, Providence permitting, I intend to be there.

A great many recollections it calls up. How many of the choice spirits have passed away!—Phillips, Hoar, Sumner, Wilson, Andrew, Hale, Chase, and others.

I remember attending the convention at Worcester, when the party was formed; and the first meeting at Tremont Temple, where I had the honor to preside, and the old hero, Giddings, gave a two-hours' address, etc., etc.

I shall be happy to meet *you*, which I have not had the pleasure of doing for quite a period, and am most truly yours,

W. B. SPOONER.

LETTER FROM NATHANIEL C. NASH, Esq.

BOSTON, August 1, 1877.

SAMUEL DOWNER, Esq.

DEAR SIR:—It gives me great pleasure to accept your kind invitation to attend the gathering in reunion of the Free-Soilers of 1848, at Melville Garden, on the 9th of August. I often look back to my early dedication to the Free-Soil party with more satisfaction than any other act of my life.

At the Free-Soil Convention held at Worcester, June 28, 1848, of which Samuel Hoar of Concord was President, the following resolution was passed, the author of which was one of the noblest of men and wisest counsellors recognized in the ranks of the old Free-Soil party, and so remained to the day of his death. Need I say that I refer to W. S. Robinson, late clerk of the House of Representatives? His noble words are as follows:—

"*Resolved*, That Massachusetts wears no chains, and spurns all bribes. Massachusetts goes now, and will ever go, for free soil and free men, for free lips and a free press, for a free land and a free world."

I remain, my dear sir, yours, very truly,

NATH'L C. NASH.

LETTER FROM THE HON. JOHN I. BAKER.

BEVERLY, August 7, 1877.

SAMUEL DOWNER, Esq.

DEAR SIR:—I have been honored with your invitation to attend the reunion of the Free-Soilers of 1848, and have delayed answering till this late moment, hoping that I might be able to accept. But circumstances beyond my control still forbid my attendance, and I am, therefore, with great reluctance, compelled to deny myself the pleasure of meeting with the many faithful friends of equal rights who will gather together on this occasion; many of whom it has been my privilege to know and to honor for these many years, and all of whom are entitled to our honor and respect for their courage and fidelity in times of trial. Trusting that you may all find rich enjoyment in review of your work in the past, and at the same time take renewed courage and hope for the right in the future, and thanking you for the invitation so kindly extended to me,

I am, with much respect,

Faithfully yours,

JOHN I. BAKER.

LETTER FROM EBENEZER CLAPP, Esq.

DORCHESTER, July 25, 1877.

DEAR FRIEND DOWNER:—I am much obliged for your cordial invitation to meet with the Free-Soilers of 1848.

How distinctly those days come before me! It may not be modest for me to say it, but I believe I was the first to make a beginning of the party which took that name. It was the day that President Taylor was nominated; it was telegraphed to Boston in the P. M. I went home; told my wife I would make a beginning of another party, if I was alone. After tea, started from the house; walked as far as Thomas Howe's, in Stoughton Street, and met Jonathan Battles; told him my business; he said he would join me. A paper was drawn up, calling a meeting, and 250 as respectable people as lived in town signed it; the list is among my papers. The first meeting was called at Lyceum Hall. You called it to order, and William Richardson, the lawyer, presided. You and I were on the committee to report resolutions; also, on the committee of vigilance. We saw the thing put through, and held on, through Know-Nothing and all other side issues, until its final triumph in 1865. We triumphed because we were on God's side; one is a majority with him.

Although very lame, I mean to be present if the weather is propitious.

Truly yours,

EBEN'R CLAPP.

LETTER FROM THE HON. HENRY CHAPIN.

SHARON SPRINGS, N. Y., July 28, 1877.

MY DEAR SIR:—Your invitation to attend a meeting of the original Free-Soilers was forwarded to me from Worcester. I suppose that I shall not return in season to attend the proposed meeting. Nothing would gratify me more than to be present. The suggestions recall to me memories which are deeply engraved in my heart. I was a member of the convention which elected Charles Allen as a delegate to the Philadelphia Convention. In our district convention, the candidates were Charles Allen and Alexander H. Bullock. It was my fortune to inform Mr. Allen that we had elected him. "Well," said he, "if you want a man uncompromisingly opposed to the extension of slavery, you have got him." You know the history of the Philadelphia Convention. Mr. Allen returned, and most of the leading Whigs turned their backs upon him. I was chairman of the Whig County Committee, and felt that Mr. Allen was right, and made up my mind, for one, to stand by him. I called the Whig County Convention, and after calling it to order, retired from the Whig party. No one, who was not in the same condition, can realize at what a sacrifice of feeling I sundered my relations with men whom I had learned to love and honor above any I had ever known; but there was a duty to be done, and from such an ordeal cowards only flinch. We were threatened with social ostracism; our names, for a time, almost cast out as evil. The last official act of Governor Clifford was to relieve me as Commissioner of Insolvency, and appoint in my place Alexander H. Bullock, afterwards Governor of Massachusetts. But time had its revenge; the stone which the builders rejected, unexpectedly to itself, became the head of the corner, and men who never expected to have any political influence were carried forward by the progress of events, until the last shackle was struck from the last slave, and the country was free from the curse of human bondage.

I have written more than I intended; but the old wheels, set in motion, will run. I doubt not that you will have a glorious time. You will have the representatives of those who believed that there was a God in Israel, and who founded a party which said what it meant, and meant what it said.

Yours truly,

HENRY CHAPIN.

LETTER FROM THE HON. R. H. DANA, JR.

BOSTON, July 28, 1877.

DEAR SIR:—I am extremely obliged to you for your kind invitation for the 9th proximo, which I should take great pleasure in accepting, but the government requires my presence at Halifax during all the month of August, before the commission there in session.

Yours, very truly,

R. H. DANA, Jr.

SAMUEL DOWNER, Esq.

LETTER FROM CHARLES M. ELLIS, ESQ.

MY DEAR MR. DOWNER:—It will give me great pleasure to join you and the other Free-Soilers of 1848 on the 9th; and, if able, I will be there, as—ever since the Latimer days of 1843, when, hating to have our State officers hired to catch slaves, and our chief justice hold court in jail, I helped get the first personal liberty bill—I have been glad to be in every pinch.

Faithfully yours,

C. M. ELLIS.

ROCKWOOD, August 1.

TELEGRAM FROM JOHN G. WHITTIER.

DANVERS, MASS., August 9, 1877.

S. DOWNER, Esq., MELVILLE GARDEN, DOWNER LANDING.

Greeting to the men of forty-eight! Thanks to the Divine Providence which has enabled us to see the end for which we labored thirty years ago! The Slave States are free. Let us draw them closer to us by generous confidence and kind offices.

JOHN G. WHITTIER.

PÆAN—1848.

By John Greenleaf Whittier.

Now, joy and thanks forevermore!
  The dreary night has well-nigh passed,
The slumbers of the North are o'er—
  The Giant stands erect at last!

More than we hoped in that dark time,
  When, faint with watching, few and worn,
We saw no welcome day-star climb
  The cold gray pathway of the morn!

O weary hours! O night of years!
  What storms our darkling pathway swept,
Where, beating back our thronging fears,
  By Faith alone our march we kept!

How jeered the scoffing crowd behind,
  How mocked before the tyrant train,
As, one by one, the true and kind
  Fell fainting in our path of pain!

They died—their brave hearts breaking slow—
  But, self-forgetful to the last,
In words of cheer and bugle blow
  Their breath upon the darkness passed.

A mighty host, on either hand,
  Stood waiting for the dawn of day
To crush like reeds our feeble band;
  The morn has come—and where are they?

Troop after troop their line forsakes;
  With peace-white banners waving free,
And from our own the glad shout breaks,
  Of Freedom and Fraternity!

Like mist before the growing light,
  The hostile cohorts melt away;
Our frowning foemen of the night
  Are brothers at the dawn of day!

As unto these repentant ones
  We open wide our toil-worn ranks,
Along our line a murmur runs
  Of song and praise and grateful thanks.

Sound for the onset! — Blast on blast!
  Till Slavery's minions cower and quail;
One charge of fire shall drive them fast
  Like chaff before our Northern gale!

O, prisoners in your house of pain,
  Dumb, toiling millions, bound and sold,
Look! stretched o'er Southern vale and plain,
  The Lord's delivering hand behold!

Above the tyrant's pride of power,
  His iron gates and guarded wall,
The bolts which shattered Shinar's tower,
  Hang, smoking, for a fiercer fall.

Awake! awake! my Father-land!
  It is thy Northern light that shines;
This stirring march of Freedom's band
  The storm-song of thy mountain pines.

Wake, dwellers where the day expires!
  And hear, in winds that sweep your lakes
And fan your prairies' roaring fires,
  The signal-call that Freedom makes!

www.ingramcontent.com/pod-product-compliance
Lightning Source LLC
Chambersburg PA
CBHW031604110426
42742CB00037B/1065